Library of
Davidson College

Psychological Testing in Personnel Assessment

First published in Great Britain by Gower Press Limited, Epping, Essex
1975

© Gower Press Limited and the authors

*Published in the U.S.A.
by Halsted Press, a Division
of John Wiley & Sons, Inc.
New York*

Library of Congress Cataloging in Publication Data
Main entry under title:

Psychological testing in personnel assessment.
 "A Halsted Press book."
 1. Ability—Testing. 2. Prediction of occupational
success. I. Miller, Kenneth M.
BF431.P8 1975   153.9'4   75-18451
ISBN 0-470-60392-5

Printed & bound in Great Britain

PSYCHOLOGICAL TESTING IN PERSONNEL ASSESSMENT

Edited by   Kenneth M. Miller

A HALSTED PRESS BOOK

JOHN WILEY & SONS
New York

Contents

Notes on Contributors	*xii*
Introduction	*xiv*

PART ONE: METHODS AND EVALUATION OF PSYCHOLOGICAL TESTING

1 Nature, advantages and limitations of psychological tests   3
  Kenneth M. Miller

Tests of general ability or intelligence	4
Tests of special abilities	5
Tests of interests and motivation	5
Assessment of personality	6
Distortion	7
Characteristics of a good test	8
Using test results	9
Making decisions	10
How to introduce tests	11
Professional and ethical considerations	12
References	15

PART TWO: CASE STUDIES IN THE USE OF PSYCHOLOGICAL TESTS

2 Introducing and validating tests: one company's experience   19

T.M. Higham
Overcoming initial opposition	20
Acceptability	22
Technical soundness	22
Validation must be repeated	24
Establishing a criterion	25
The classic approach	27
Hints on using tests	27

3 Use of tests in the Post Office Corporation — 29

W.A. Furness
Psychological tests for postmen?	29
Reasons for using tests	30
Tests for selection at below-management levels	31
Tests for selection at managerial levels	32
Tests for promotion	34
Concept of the assessment centre	34
Case for including tests and other exercises in promotion procedures	35
Some current uses of tests in promotion procedures	35
Validation	36
Tests in use — some practical considerations	41

4 Use of tests at United Biscuits — 45

D. Wilson
Procedure for testing during selection	45
General approach of the company to testing	46
Company policy	47
Graduate recruitment	48
Management development	49
Supervisory selection and development from within the company	52
Other uses of tests	56
Additional benefits from the use of tests	56
Introduction of tests	57
Conclusions	59

5 Graduate selection — 61

C.C.P. Ingleton
Selection procedure	61
Current testing procedure	63
Problems encountered	64
Reaction of line managers to tests	66
Reaction of graduates to tests	66
Motivational distortion	69
Evaluation of tests	70
Summary	75
References	75

6	The use of tests and scored questionnaires in salesmen selection	77
	G.A. Randell	
	Collecting the data	78
	Tests and questionnaires used	79
	Analysing the data	80
	Findings and outcomes	80
	General conclusions	88
	References	90
7	Selecting engineers in an electronics firm	91
	J. Copeland	
	The Morrisby Differential Test Battery	93
	Other tests	99
	Using the tests	100
	Contribution from the DTB	103
	Future plans	106
	Conclusion	106
	References	107
8	Choosing tests for clerical selection	109
	Kenneth M. Miller	
	Purposes of the study	109
	Samples	110
	Criterion measures	112
	Contribution of each individual test	112
	Best combination of tests	116
	Effectiveness	119
	Conclusion	121
9	Use of tests for local authority staff	122
	J. Gibson	
	Difficulties in selection peculiar to local authorities	122
	Decision to use tests	124
	Purposes for which tests are used	125
	Staff assessed by tests	125
	The tests and their contribution	127
	Future developments	133
	References	135
10	Use of tests in a national retail company	137
	R. Beaton	
	Factors influencing the introduction of tests	137
	Objectives	138
	Situations in which one type of criterion only	

was suitable	139
Situations in which the one criterion was not categorical but continuous	142
Situations in which more than one type of criterion is applied	145
Situations in which personality is 'suited' to a job	147
Contribution of tests to Telefusion's selection procedure	148

PART THREE: SURVEY OF THE USE OF PSYCHOLOGICAL TESTS

11 The use of tests in British industry and commerce — 151

Kenneth M. Miller

Description of the sample	152
Use of tests	154
Information about individual members of the IPM	162
Summary and implications	163
Postcript	164
Reference	165

PART FOUR: APPENDICES

Appendix 1 British Psychological Society criteria for evaluating short training courses on psychological tests	169
Appendix 2 Tests referred to in Part Two *J. Gibson*	171
Index	177

Illustrations

Figure
1:1 Appraisal of an individual 4

3:1 Numbers recruited by the Post Office in various grades in 1974 30
3:2 Rating of 'intellectual qualities' 38
3:3 Relationship between grade in an apprentice selection test and success in a public examination 40

4:1 Stages in group selection programme for marketing trainees 48
4:2 16PF and AH6 results for 50 middle managers attending company assessment centres (average age 35) 50
4:3 Mean Sten scores on primary and second-order factors on 16PF and AH4 scores for first-line supervisors in five factories 54
4:4 Correlation between peer and boss assessments of success and personal characteristics of supervisors in five factories 55

5:1 Initial test battery 62
5:2 Typical applicant's timetable for second interview 64
5:3 Procedure for estimating the 'probability' of an

	applicant accepting or declining a job offer from his 16PF scores	73
7:1	A typical DTB profile	94
7:2	Four basic profiles from the ability block of the DTB	95
7:3	Indications of general approach to tasks	97
7:4	Modal profiles: basic modes of probable mental behaviour predicted by the first four speed tests	98
7:5	Profiles from the dexterity speed tests	99
7:6	Profile of an applicant for a student apprenticeship	100
7:7	Profile of a perfectionist	102
8:1	Groups of tests suggested for two users	111
8:2	Correlation between test scores and performance	113
8:3	Mean scores and percentile equivalents on Survey of Interpersonal Values for insurance sample	114
8:4	Mean scores and percentile equivalents on Survey of Personal Values for mail order sample	115
8:5	Expectancy chart: PTI-Verbal and Arithmetic	117
8:6	Expectancy chart: PTI-Verbal, Arithmetic and Filing	117
8:7	Expectancy chart: PTI-Verbal, Arithmetic, Filing, Coding	118
8:8	Phi values for the mail order sample	
8:9	Correlation between test scores and training grades	120
9:1	Purposes for which tests are used by local authorities	126
9:2	Tests used by local authorities	129
10.1	Expectancy charts for AH4 and ACER Mechanical Reasoning Tests indicating percentage chances of passing Trade Test for group 1 (technical trainees)	140
10:2	Actual and predicted results achieved by group 2 (technical trainees) in Trade Test	141
10:3	Relationship between AH4, Mechanical Reasoning Test and pass or fail in Trade Test for groups 1 and 2 combined (technical trainees)	142
10:4	Technical trainees	144
10:5	Relationship between PTI-V scores and performances for sales staff	146
10:6	Efficiencies of various criteria for selecting branch managers	148
11:1	The sample by category of industry and use or	

	nonuse of tests	153
11:2	Selection procedures	155
11:3	Frequency of use of number of selection procedures	156

Notes on Contributors

Kenneth M. Miller (Editor) is Director of the Independent Assessment and Research Centre which carries out a broad programme of assessment, research and training. He started his career teaching, before taking up a post as Psychologist within the Civil Service Research Unit. Dr. Miller began lecturing at University College, London, before moving to the University of Tasmania. He then undertook research within the Psychology Department at UCL and NFER. Before taking up his present position he became Director of the Research Unit at the School Examinations Department, University of London. Dr. Miller is a Fellow of the British Psychological Society, of the Australian Psychological Society and, currently, Chairman of the BPS Standing Committee on Test Standards.

R. Beaton (Use of tests in a national retail company) is Group Personnel Manager for Telefusion Limited, where he has spent most of his career. He is a Governor of Oldham College of Technology and occasional Lecturer at the Lancastria School of Management.

J. Copeland (Selecting engineers in an electronics firm) has had many years of experience within the engineering industry, the last fifteen being spent in Training. He is

Chairman of the Engineering Advisory Committee, and a Member of the St. Albans College of Further Education, Engineering Advisory Committee. Mr. Copeland is a Fellow of the Institute of Training Officers.

W.A. Furness (Use of tests in the Post Office Corporation) is Head of Surveys and Special Projects Group in the Psychological Services Division within the Post Office Corporation. He spent two years in full-time post-graduate study in occupation psychology at Birkbeck College, London University, before becoming Senior Psychologist within the Post Office Corporation.

J.N. Gibson (Use of tests for local authority staff) is a Director of Behavioural Sciences Consultants. He has had experience as a Training Officer with London County Council and the National Coal Board and is an Occupational Psychologist, a personnel consultant and Lecturer in Management Studies.

T.M. Higham (Introducing and validating tests: one company's experience) is Recruitment Manager with Rowntree Mackintosh Limited, Director and Chairman of the Roffey Park Institute Limited and Director of the Standing Conference of Employers of Graduates Limited. He is an Associate of the British Psychological Society and a Fellow of the Institute of Personnel Management.

C.C.P. Ingleton (Graduate selection) is Lecturer in Occupational Psychology in the Department of Business Studies at the University of Edinburgh. Formerly he was a Research Assistant at the University of Bradford Management Centre. Mr. Ingleton is a Graduate member of both the Institute of Personnel Management and the British Psychological Society.

G.A. Randell (The use of tests and scored questionnaires in salesmen selection) is Senior Lecturer in Occupational Psychology at the University of Bradford Management Centre. He is a consultant in management development, Chairman of IARC and Assessor to the Civil Service Selection Board.

D. Wilson (Use of tests at United Biscuits) is Group Training Development Manager of United Biscuits Limited. He has worked in consultancy, holds a first degree in Science and is a Member of the Institute of Personnel Management.

Introduction

The importance of psychological testing is not always fully understood by personnel managers. This book has therefore been designed as a non-technical guide to the purpose of tests and how they are used in practice.

Part One is a brief presentation of information necessary for the reader to obtain a general background against which to appreciate the case studies in Part Two. The authors were invited to contribute because they use psychological tests as an integral part of their work with a wide range of staff, in industry, business or commerce.

The format of each case study differs slightly according to the experience or the situations being described. Nevertheless all authors have indicated why the organizations began using tests, describe some of the situations in which tests are used and have commented on the effectiveness of tests. In all case studies some statistical information is given to support the evaluative conclusions. This information ranges from simple desk-calculated indices to more sophisticated computer-based analyses. Information about these techniques can be obtained from the references at the end of the introduction.

Part Three is a summary of a survey of the use of tests in British industry which indicates the wide and increasing use of tests throughout the whole of the industrial and commercial fields.

The aim of preparing this book will have been fulfilled if the enquiring reader has been helped to reach a decision as to whether his organization would benefit from the introduction of psychological tests in personnel work and at the same time has gained an appreciation of the limitations as well as advantages.

REFERENCES

Miller, Robert B. (1968), *Statistical Concepts and Applications,* (Chicago: SRA)

Guilford, J.P. *Fundamental Statistics in Psychology and Education,* 4th edition (New York: McGraw Hill)

Part One

Methods and Evaluation of Psychological Testing

1

Nature, Advantages and Limitations of Psychological Tests

Kenneth M. Miller

Any personnel officer or line manager wanting to make a new appointment or to recommend a member of present staff for promotion is better able to do this if he has comprehensive answers to three questions:

1 Can this person do the job or be trained to do it?
2 Will he be interested in doing it?
3 How will he go about it?

Psychological tests are not the only way of appraising an individual and obtaining an answer to these questions. Figure 1:1 summarizes the sources of information available for assessing various aspects of an individual's personality and abilities. The sectors in the figure will have varying importance for different jobs though for some positions the selector will have to consider all sectors. The appraiser who does not use tests to provide information will have to fall back on other methods, notably interviewing.

Standardized tests provide comparable, objective information about all the candidates for a single position, whereas in the interview it is difficult to
_____
I am indebted to John Gibson for reading through the first draft of this chapter and making several suggestions which I have incorporated in the final version.

Figure 1:1 Appraisal of an individual

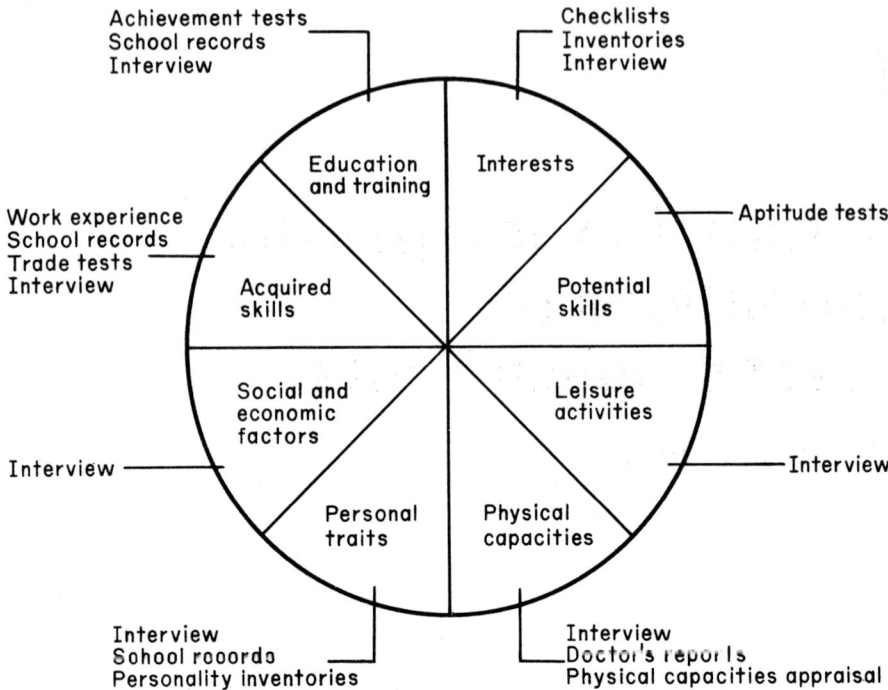

separate objective information from subjective impression. Much has been written about the unreliability of interviews but less about the single most important factor contributing to unreliability: the lack of adequate training in interviewing technique.

TESTS OF GENERAL ABILITY OR INTELLIGENCE

The first question, 'Can he do it?' can be answered partially by looking at information about education, training and experience, and all such information can be gained without recourse to psychological tests. The picture can be completed by using some of the many tests which have been developed to assess basic abilities and aptitudes. A knowledge of results from tests of this kind can make two important contributions: the decision-maker has comparable information for all candidates and he has it on attributes which are less subject to (in some cases almost devoid of) educational and experiential influences.

Tests of general ability are either 'omnibus' or designed to assess only one component of ability.

In the omnibus type items or questions covering all

aspects of intelligence are presented in a single test and yield either an overall index or part scores for the different components represented, such as verbal, numerical and nonverbal. Sometimes a total score or overall index is obtained by combining the part scores. Most of the test distributors listed at the end of the book have one or more of these types of tests in their catalogues. One of the best known of the omnibus type was the Otis test which recently has been rebuilt and now appears as BEST (Basic Employee Selection Test).

Examples of tests that assess only one main component of general ability are the Raven's Progressive Matrices Test which has only nonverbal or diagrammatic items and the General Ability Test - Verbal, which is part of the Differential Test Battery, and consists entirely of verbal items.

TESTS OF SPECIAL ABILITIES

The two main special abilities are mechanical and spatial, sometimes referred to as technical/practical abilities. A fairly high level of either or both of these is necessary for a person to be successful in fields like engineering, architecture, design or dentistry.

Other psychological areas for which tests have been developed include manual or motor dexterity, perceptual speed and memory. Perusal of a general textbook on personnel testing, such as Guion (1965) or Lawshe and Balma (1966), will give a fuller appreciation of the range of ability and aptitude areas for which tests have been developed.

TESTS OF INTERESTS AND MOTIVATION

If the answer to the first question, 'Can he do it?' is affirmative the answers to the next two questions become relevant. If the answer has been clearly negative the other two questions are unlikely to be asked.

Information to answer the question, 'Will he do it?' comes from the areas of interest and motivation. Again skilful interviewing can elicit useful answers. However, vocational interest questionnaires, which establish an order of preference for occupational fields or the similarity of an individual to a sample of successful people in a particular career, are available and allow the information to be obtained more directly and systematically.

Interests which have persisted over several years form an important component of a person's motivation. A further component is the amount of energy a person is prepared to devote to those interests. The objectives behind such interests and energy expended also characterize motives. Some seek job satisfaction, some riches, some prestige, some seek regularity and family happiness, others seek adventure. Some like to work with money, others with people or a particular kind of commodity ('My heart has always been in groceries' said one young lady with enthusiasm). To many, the challenge of science and technology or of art and literature is irresistible.

Also in the same general area are surveys of values or attitude/motivational scales. These ascertain whether, for example, the support of other people or being in a leadership position or having freedom to plan one's own work are seen as being important by the individual.

The assumption here is that even though a person may have an appropriate pattern and level of abilities he will only be fully effective in the job if he is interested in the field of work for which he is suited and the working conditions are congenial for him.

ASSESSMENT OF PERSONALITY

Even if the first two questions are answered affirmatively it could happen that one person's usual or typical way of approaching problems and interacting with other people could make him a good prospect for a particular job under consideration, whereas another person with the same pattern of abilities and interests may be not a good prospect because his temperament or personality is likely to hinder his work in that particular job - but not necessarily in a similar position or with another company.

The most frequently used method for assessing personality in personnel work is the self-report questionnaire. The Eysenck Personality Inventory, the Cattell 16 Personality Factor Questionnaire, the Gordon Personal Profile and Personal Inventory and the Guildford-Zimmerman Temperament Survey are the ones most often used in industry. Other approaches to the assessment of personality, such as the Rorschach inkblot test, are usually more time-consuming and require a full psychological training for their use and interpretation. These devices, except in rare cases, are not used in industry.

Sometimes a sample of behaviour, which is not standardized in the same way as a questionnaire, is obtained. An example is the leaderless group task situation used in the Army officer selection procedure and sometimes in group selection procedures adopted by larger companies or external assessment centres. The effective use of this type of procedure is dependent upon the training of the assessors.

The different questionnaires have been developed to provide either a very broad or a fine description of personality. The Eysenck Personality Inventory provides information about extraversion-introversion and about anxiety-adjustment. At the other end of the range the Cattell 16PF elicits information about 16 basic factors and, from scores on these, broader patterns are derived. For some personnel purposes information about a few broad factors is sufficient but for others information from the more narrowly defined traits is desirable.

DISTORTION

What is the likelihood of a respondent distorting or 'faking good' his responses to personality questionnaires? The overall answer is much less than might be expected. That this is so is due largely to the way in which the psychologist or suitably trained non-psychologist tester introduces the questionnaire to the respondent. The need to handle the test situation effectively is one of the reasons why the use of personality assessment methods is carefully controlled.

With two-factor questionnaires it would be easier to distort responses to fit a preconceived idea of what was required for a particular job. With complex multiple-factor questionnaires it is more difficult to know what is required and to be effective in selecting the 'right' responses.

Most consultants and many companies assessing professional and managerial applicants offer, before the testing begins, to provide 'feedback' on the test performance. This in itself has been found to minimize distortion in replies to personality and motivation questionnaires.

A fuller discussion on this issue is to be found in

Anastasi (1968) or in Ungerson (1975).

CHARACTERISTICS OF A GOOD TEST

Before they are published all tests should have met certain technical standards usually laid down by the psychological profession in the country of origin. These technical elements are briefly described below.

Objectivity
This book is concerned only with tests which can be described as objective - in other words, tests in which there is no subjectivity attached to the scoring or the interpretation of the response. In a test of maximum ability there is only one right or wrong answer for each question. For each question in the personality inventory, the individual makes a choice of one of two or three alternatives and the author has predetermined that a particular alternative belongs to a particular trait or characteristic. It is not for the person who scores the test to make decisions about the meaning of the answers.

Reliability
Any test must be seen as obtaining or assessing a sample of behaviour. The test user needs to have confidence that the sample is a representative one and that testees will perform in much the same way whenever they are tested. This consistency of measurement is basically what is meant by reliability. Put in another way it concerns the degree of 'error' or tolerance attached to the result. Various factors, such as inappropriate or poor administration of the test, can influence reliability. The test author has an obligation to provide data about reliability in the manual or handbook for the test.

Validity
There are various types of validity which might concern a test user but in the industrial setting it is nearly always predictive validity that matters, in other words, how well do scores on a test relate to performance on the job?
   The first problem in this situation is what is meant by performance? Does it mean overall general performance or does it mean certain elements of performance? Reference to most textbooks will show that

elements of performance can usually be predicted rather better than overall or global performance. A comprehensive survey by Ghiselli (1966) covering a period of 40 years of reports on the usefulness of tests showed that in nearly all cases the addition of psychological tests had improved selection.

While reliability can be taken to be fairly general for a particular test, validity needs checking out in different situations. The specific work setting, or the methods for doing what is called the same job in two companies, can influence the effectiveness of tests as aids to selection.

The validity of a test is also dependent to some extent upon factors such as the proportion of applicants being selected for occupations and the proportion of people already doing the job judged to be successful.

Demonstrated predictive usefulness can help in selecting trial tests for a new situation and, if replicated often enough in a wide sample of companies, can give confidence about usefulness in a new project.

USING TEST RESULTS

Psychological test results can be used in three ways: to predict, to compare and to understand. In the personnel field it has traditionally been the first of these that has been involved. The basic assumption has been that the higher a score on a single test or a total score derived from several tests, or the more appropriate the pattern of scores on several tests, the more effective will be the person in the job.

This assumption is always subject to the proviso that in some jobs there can be a level above which the person would be too good for the work, would become bored and would therefore be inefficient or would perhaps stay only a short time.

In the cases of personality and interest measures, where as many as 16 factors are assessed, there has often been the illusory search for a perfect profile against which all applicants would be compared. A more fruitful approach can be to ascertain which set of factors from the larger number is most important and/or to establish limits of acceptability. For example, in the case of air traffic controllers only five of the Cattell factors are really important.

Even if no evidence is available about the predictive effectiveness of a personality or cognitive test the availability of a comprehensive set of test scores provides useful systematic information about a person. One very experienced psychologist in British industry has stated that in an hour of pencil-and-paper personality testing he can obtain information about a person which would otherwise require at least six weeks of close and careful observation of the person in all types of situations - even if such observation could be carried out. This fuller knowledge of the person is most useful in the case of managers and professional staff where positions are usually few and the criteria of job performance hard to obtain with the consequent difficulty of carrying out a traditional validity study. The fuller information gained by tests helps the personnel manager compare several applicants. The third use, to understand a person, comes about when test results may help a manager to obtain some guidance on why a member of staff has not been performing particularly well. If a clerical officer is frequently having difficulty with accuracy of figure work, then a test may reveal that this individual has a very low numerical ability and would be much better placed in a different situation, perhaps filing or general clerical duties. Understanding of this kind also comes from effective use of personality questionnaires where some particular aspect of the individual's personal characheristics might be hampering him in the performance of his job. This third use of tests does require the user to have rather more sophistication and basic underlying knowledge than do the previous two.

MAKING DECISIONS

In any selection or promotion situation decisions are made in terms of probabilities. When a personnel manager recommends and a line manager makes an appointment, they are saying it is probable that the particular candidate will do the job more effectively than any other candidate. Very often considerable careful weighing-up will have been done, for seldom is the matching between man characteristics and job characteristics perfect or even very good.
All items of information must play their part. When psychological tests have been used there is sometimes a tendency to disregard all other information. This practice is faulty on two grounds:

1 Although tests, if they are appropriate and an adequate number have been given, do provide comparable information, that information is not necessarily or even usually more important than other data.
2 It is false to assume that tests are perfect and the test score is a fixed measure. Human beings are not consistent and tests are not perfect, so a test score has certain limitations, but within these a very useful contribution can be made.

At what point should test results be introduced into the selection process? Without going into the extensive arguments on this question it can be noted that some people prefer not to know the test results of someone who is being interviewed in case the interview should be biased by the knowledge. Others feel that having the test results available enables more relevant questions to be asked in a final interview.

HOW TO INTRODUCE TESTS

The effective use of tests in many ways depends on the first step: that of determining which tests are most appropriate - that is, most job-related. Job-relatedness can refer to particular behaviour or work in the job but it can also mean having sufficient level of particular abilities to be taught the job.

The more comprehensive and precise the initial analysis can be the quicker will be the payoff. Many companies will benefit from calling on outside help for this stage. If they do not, and rely on a member of staff to execute this aspect after a basic course in psychological testing, then the development time is likely to be longer although the course should have given sufficient guidance for work to begin.

On the basis of either a concurrent validity or a predictive validity study the group of tests to be used will be refined and usually shortened. Once a test battery has been arrived at it is necessary to see that administration and interpretation standards are maintained. Test administration can be time-consuming and once a personnel officer has become reasonably skilled it is possible to consider training less highly qualified staff to administer and score the tests. Secretaries and senior clerical assistants have good records as 'sergeant' testers. It is necessary, however, to have these people trained properly and not just told what to do by the personnel officer.

As a concurrent validity study will very often have been the initial study it is necessary also to carry out a predictive validity study and to repeat it on at least one further occasion to provide cross-validation.

From time to time modifications of the job or the process may require the personnel department to revise its assessment procedures.

PROFESSIONAL AND ETHICAL CONSIDERATIONS

Test suppliers frequently receive a request from a personnel officer who has just become convinced that psychological tests are something he should have been using and writes immediately to order some tests. If he has written to a recognized test distributor or publisher he will receive back a qualification form to complete. This form is designed to obtain information about his general education and training and in particular about his training in the administration of tests and interpretation of test scores.

Very often the next letter will be to tell him that he does not, at present, qualify to purchase any tests of ability-aptitude, interest or personality and will recommend that he obtain appropriate training. An alternative would be to enlist the services of an occupational psychologist who can carry out the work for him.

If he decides to undertake training there are several organizations which have organized courses for different levels of testing. These courses will have been planned according to a series of guidelines drawn up by the British Psychological Society at the request of the test suppliers and approved by the Standing Committee on Test Standards and the council of the British Psychological Society.

Tests are graded according to the difficulty of interpretation and the amount of psychological background required to handle the concepts. Somewhat ironically the more difficult the interpretation the less difficult the actual administration.

Ability and aptitude tests usually can be introduced in a five-day course with various supplementary courses to extend the range and type of test. Personality test courses require the student first to have had training in ability and aptitude tests and experience in using them. Specific and fairly stringent course follow-up is required for personality tests.

Unfortunately, some organizations, which do not employ psychologists, have special personality measures which they are willing to distribute on less stringent conditions than those adopted by professional psychological organizations. As the untrained personnel officer does not realize the need to ask about the reliability and validity of these instruments, the necessary evidence is seldom produced and the authors of these measures seldom bother to report on them in professional or scientific journals, and thus make them available for worthwhile evaluation and criticism. Obviously, tests of this sort should be regarded with some caution.

Test results
The method of reporting on test results also requires careful adherence to professional standards. Courses on testing stress this aspect along with the confidentiality of test scores.

Ethical considerations
British professional bodies are somewhat reluctant to lay down detailed rules on ethical matters with specific examples, preferring to treat cases as they arise. At present, the British Psychological Society adopts this *ad hoc* approach. However, there are moves to follow the American Psychological Association's practice of laying down a code of ethics with very specific illustrative examples. In the United States of America the professional body has frequently invoked this code to discipline erring members. Even so, psychological tests are widely used by personnel staff who are not psychologists and examples of misuse are found. Yet it was not specific examples of misuse that caused a major upheaval in the use of psychological tests but rather a widespread neglect to follow up the usefulness of tests.

In 1964 the Civil Rights Act was passed by the US Congress. The Act turned its attention to any procedure which might be unfair to minority groups. However, the Act did not require intent to be proved, for its force to be applied. The inference was made (probably correct in some cases) that some companies were using psychological tests not as a means of appraising their level of intake or success in selection but rather as a way of excluding members of minority groups.

In essence the Act required that all selection
prodedures be:
1 Specifically related to job requirements
2 Fair and reasonable
3 Administered in good faith
4 Properly evaluated
5 Professionally developed
6 Not used as the sole determining factor

So far, court cases arising from the Act have been mainly concerned with tests though the Act is written in such a way that non-test procedures, such as unscored interviews and application forms, should also meet the same requirements.

One ruling by the legal commission on a complaint brought against a company summarizes the situation neatly. Because this company had a history of discrimination prior to passage of the Act and because the start of testing coincided with the lowering of race barriers, the commission felt it had reasonable grounds for labelling the use of such tests suspect. The commission ruled that the company had failed to show that:

> The traits measured by these tests are traits which are necessary for the successful performance of the specific jobs available at Respondent's plant. Nor does it appear that any of the tests have been validated properly in terms of the specific jobs available at Respondent's work force. In the absence of evidence that the tests are properly related to the jobs and have been properly validated, Respondent has no rational basis for believing that employees and applicants who pass the test will make more successful employees than those who fail; conversely, Respondent has no rational basis for believing that employees and applicants who fail the test will not make successful employees. Respondent's testing procedures, therefore, are not 'professionally developed'.

As a result of the Civil Rights Act and the later Equal Employment Oppurtunities Act, guidelines for the use of tests in selection were drawn up by the Equal Employmer Opportunities Commission. Two supreme court cases have had particular bearing on these. In Griggs versus Duke Power Company it was decided EEOC guidelines were entitled to respect, though they were not, in fact, law. In particular it was insisted that selection test results must be validated against an acceptable measure of job performance. In a very recent case (1975) against the Albermarle Paper Company the need for all employees to follow the guidelines was further emphasised.

Although there is, to date, no evidence of companies in the UK using tests to discriminate against members of minority groups it is essential that British companies be aware of the situation which developed in the USA. Byham and Spitzer (1971) have done much more than spell out the legal implications. They have also produced a very clearly written guide which describes for the newcomer what essential professional steps should be taken when introducing tests. Provision in terms of sufficient staff or finance to call on outside help must be made if tests are to be introduced effectively.

REFERENCES

Anastasi, Anne (1968), *Psychological Testing*, 3rd edition (New York: Collier-Macmillan)

Byham, W.E. & Spitzer, M.E. (1971), *The Law and Personnel Testing* (London: Allen & Unwin Ltd)

Ghiselli, E.E. (1966), *The Validity of Occupational Aptitude Tests* (New York: Wiley)

Guion, R.M. (1965), *Personnel Testing* (New York: McGraw-Hill)

Lawshe, C.H. & Balma, M.J. (1966), *Principles of Personnel Testing*, 2nd edition (New York: McGraw-Hill)

Ungerson, B. (ed) (1975), *Recruitment Handbook*, 2nd edition (Epping: Gower Press)

Part Two

Case Studies in the Use of Psychological Tests

2

Introducing and Validating Tests: One company's experience

T. M. Higham

Fifty years ago, Rowntree's comparatively newly formed and recently recognized clerks' union passed a resolution, pledging its members to resist scientific management in general and the activities of the company's equally newly formed psychological department in particular. Times have changed; today it is certain that APEX (as they are now) would object if for some reason our standard selection practice, which includes psychological tests and interviews, was not followed. But in 1924 it was a different matter, for then the psychological department was but a stripling infant two years old, just beginning to stand on its own two feet.

The decision to start such a department in the first place sprang from Seebohm Rowntree's work with the Ministry of Munitions during the First World War. He had seen there something of the value of systematic selection methods, and decided that he would like to introduce them at the factory. His decision met some opposition, which was not surprising, but this was eventually overcome.

OVERCOMING INITIAL OPPOSITION

It might be as well, at this point, to look back and see just how the opposition was overcome. The company had set up a system of formal joint consultation in 1919, and Seebohm Rowntree's suggestion of appointing a psychologist to administer and interpret tests was put formally to a meeting of the council; they rejected it. But he did not give up. Over the next year or so, he invited a number of prominent psychologists (notably the late Sir Cyril Burt, and the late Professor Tom Pear) to come and talk to the council about tests and testing; eventually the council agreed to give the idea a try, but they added two provisos: first, the psychologist's activities were to be answerable to a worker-management committee; second, the psychologist was to be appointed from within the company. Both potential stumbling blocks were eventually got round. The department started work and after about two years the supervising committee decided that it could exist in its own right.

The elements - the significant steps - in the introduction of tests and testing, were four:

1 Consultation with representatives of those on whom the tests would be used.
2 Full information about tests was made available to those representatives.
3 An element of control over the scope of testing was introduced until the company was satisfied that such control was not needed.
4 Lastly care was taken over the appointment of the tester.

Times may have changed but those four elements would still seem to me to be essential; exactly how the control element would be introduced will obviously vary from organization to organization but I am sure that in the early stages the scope of testing would need to be carefully watched by, say, a sympathetic manager who was himself aware of what tests could or could not do.

For tests to be generally accepted throughout a company will take a longer time. A psychological department is by its nature a service department, with an advisory function. It has, to use Paterson's term, sapiential authority, which he defines as the entitlement to be heard by reason of special knowledge or expertness; but that authority is vested, not in the job but in the person doing it; in short it needs to be earned and that is only likely to happen after some time, when the results of using tests in selection are seen to be justified, and the department giving them has also established a reputation generally for being fair and impartial.

Tests are often strange or even frightening when first encountered by people who are not used to them. Even today care has to be taken to explain why tests are used and for what purpose. The first psychologists at Rowntree's were well aware of that and, to a large extent, it determined the choice of tests used.

Almost all the tests were of performance, analogous with jobs done in the factory. Some called for hand and eye coordination, for correctness and rhythm, or for rudimentary practical abilities as displayed, for example, on a formboard. Some paper-and-pencil tests were designed for office use — for the clerks' objection had somehow been overcome — but those tests were really attainment tests. In 1946 we introduced a sorting, checking, classifying type test (related to our industry), with a test of mathematics and one of general intelligence.

The original factory performance tests took nearly an hour to administer. Paper-and-pencil tests were not used mainly because, for most factory applicants and existing staff, it was a long time since they had left school and in any case such tests were felt to put them at a disadvantage. The original performance tests were still in use in 1948 and three of the original sixteen are in occasional use today.

The department has always insisted on validating its tests not only to see if they actually measure what they are supposed to measure but also to see if, as measuring instruments, they are effective and trustworthy. When thirteen of the orginal tests were dropped in 1948 it was because the other three (plus one new one) gave a more consistent measure of what was wanted; they also took less time to administer than the original battery of tests.

The technical soundness of tests and their administrative convenience are two of the three criteria of systematic selection which were suggested by Professor Alec Rodger in 1949, when he was writing about the eleven-plus selection. His third criterion was 'political defensibility' which was appropriate enough in the circumstances; it could be translated today into 'general acceptability': and technical soundness, ease of administration and acceptability are still essential in any selection programme.

ACCEPTABILITY

Much of the early opposition to tests at Rowntree's was overcome when factory staff found that they were doing jobs they could learn to do well and at which they earned good money, rather than finding, after a few weeks, that they were never likely to reach full efficiency. That pleased management as well and the failure rate among packers was cut from 20 to 5 per cent over 18 months. Better still, from an acceptability point of view, the union took up the case of several men who were to be dismissed for incompetence, suggesting that they might have been wrongly placed at the start. Could they not be tested to see what jobs they were more suitable for? They were and some of them were kept and given jobs more in line with their talents and temperament and in which they rapidly made good (but whether because of the effectiveness of the tests or the second chance they were given is difficult to say). There was little opposition after that, and any that there was seems rapidly to have disappeared after the Second World War when men and women grew accustomed to taking tests of ability and aptitude in the Services.

Mild opposition may still be encountered, usually from younger graduates or professional men who believe that a BA or a BSc, a CA or an ARIC is a guarantee, if not of a high IQ, at least of competence on the job and that their degree or professional qualifications has, by some strange magic, put them above the rest of mankind.

However vital convenience of administration and general acceptability may be, in the long run a selection programme stands or falls on its technical competence: in other words, does it measure what it is meant to measure and are its measurements consistent?

TECHNICAL SOUNDNESS

The consistency or reliability of a test is relatively easy to determine simply by means of testing and retesting the same group of people. A test would not normally be put on the market by a reputable organization or publisher unless it was reliable in its measurements. The group that is tested or retested and, more important still, the group whose performance is later compared against test scores to see if the test predicts good performance must be large if the results are to be meaningful at all; there must be a good 'sample' of the 'population' - whether the population as a whole or of the localized 'population' of a particular department, division or organization.

The problem is that it usually takes a long time to collect information on a sample that is large enough to validate the test properly. There is an additional difficulty: most firms test more than they employ. If 130 graduates are tested for 20 vacancies then it is only possible as a rule to follow up the 20, and very difficult to find what has happened to the other 110. If tests are used to weed out unsuitable applicants then there is no indication of how they might have done - unless the organization takes the risk of employing them in order to compare later performance with the original test results.

It took Rowntree's ten years to collect enough efficiency assessments and production results to compare against scores on two performance tests for women in the factory even though the jobs in question (packing and decorating chocolates) were ones for which there was a steady demand. That was because it was necessary to allow for training time and experience before getting the efficiency ratings, and in that time internal transfers, work changes, leavers, changes on marriage from full to part-time work, sickness absence and many other variables effectively reduced the total number needed for a constant sample, i.e. for a controlled follow-up which would satisfy statistical criteria.

Although it is difficult to validate the tests used for selecting factory staff, where objective measures of output can often be used for comparison, that is an easy task compared with trying to validate tests used for office, sales or management staff selection.

Certainly, for a job with a set training period at the end of which there is a test of skill - as in typing, comptometer or punch operating, or programming — it is possible to use tests to select trainees. Rowntree's experience and that of the Armed Forces in the war showed convincingly that tests could help in the selection of trainees. In general, for many trades in the Services, a test performance above a certain level was a good indication of ability to learn (if not of motivation). Occasionally it was - and is - possible to be

precise and say that a candidate with a test score
below a certain level is almost certainly not likely to
be able to do a certain job. That does not mean that
someone scoring above that level will do it success-
fully: only that they have the ability to do it, just
as the score below it means that they lack the basic
ability, however willing or keen they may be.

Perhaps the classic example of this cutoff score was
seen in the RNVR. All officer candidates after 1942
were tested and the test results were compared with the
final course marks at the Officer Training Establishment,
HMS King Alfred. In a group of 415 cadet ratings, 39
obtained 800 marks or more on the course. None of these
had scored fewer than 110 marks in the intelligence test
given previously. At the other end of the scale 55,
that is 86 per cent, of the 64 men who scored 600 marks
or less on the course were found to have obtained intelligence test marks below 110. That meant in practice that a
candidate for a commission who scored only 105 marks in
the test was very likely, if he survived the course at
all, to get a poor pass. It meant too that his chance
of being in the top flight, among those who are awarded
800 marks or more, was virtually nil.

This does not necessarily imply that those with the
highest scores made the best officers. There was of
course some overlap: high test scores, low course marks
and vice versa. However, a very similar result was
found in the other Services, suggesting that an intelligence level somewhere in the top 10 per cent of the
population was needed to become an officer. In much the
same way the average or mean scores on a twenty-minute
test of verbal intelligence, given to foremen, charge-
hands and leading hands in the factory were significantly
different, i.e. it was most unlikely that this was a
chance finding. There were real differences between the
three groups. But here again there was much overlapping
so that the brightest leading hands were as intelligent
as some of the foremen. One of the great difficulties
with cut-off scores is that some will be taken on who,
although bright enough, will not make the grade and some
who, though thick, will.

VALIDATION MUST BE REPEATED

Another difficulty is that validation is rarely a once-
and-for-all affair. For example, some years ago we
tried to find out whether successful salesmen had any-

thing in common which marked them off from the less successful ones. We tabulated, for each group, such items as type of school, 'O' levels, leadership experience, selling experience, social interests, test score and marital status. There were only two items which did differentiate significantly (i.e. better than chance): test score and marital status. Whether it was that the brighter ones got married sooner or that the combination of the two provided an indirect measure of some social skill needed in selling I shall not try to guess. However, over the next few years, the nature of selling in our business changed a great deal and later research has not substantiated the earlier findings.

That may have been, in part, because the criterion (an assessment of success on the job) was not a very objective one in the first place. The volume of sales could be used as a criterion, but how can allowance be made for differences in area, type of retail outlet, and business generally? Almost inevitably, it is necessary to use a subjective rating, either by, say, an area or divisional sales manager, which might be unreliable, or by some head office sales director who could at least coordinate views and make allowances for severe or over-kind markings - which was the first method we used.

ESTABLISHING A CRITERION

The setting up of a criterion and the elimination of variables are the most difficult parts of validating a test.

As an illustration of the difficulties of validation, consider the recruitment of graduates and younger professional men. A test score is needed as part of the selection process in order to get a measure against which achievements in other spheres can be compared - e.g. class of degree, examination results or level of interests. For it is the whole or total pattern which is the main concern in selection.

For fifteen years, we had used a twenty-minute verbal intelligence test which we had devised, standardized and validated - the same test, in fact, that was used in the studies of salesmen and supervisors referred to just now. But with graduates a snag appeared: a range of only one mark separated the top 5 per cent from the next 15 per cent and only two marks separated that 15 per cent from the middle 40 per cent. With other groups the spread was better and, if the scores of all those tested were put together, there was a normal distribution.

Since then we have used two tests; the first one is still being validated while the second awaits even the start of a validation study.

There have been no problems with candidates who are asked to take the tests; some managers may have been expecting the tests to produce a magic formula which would guarantee success or failure. We have had to point out that the norms we quote to them were for graduates and that an 'E-score' merely meant that student was in the bottom 10 per cent of the graduate population as a whole, and - because we were still experimenting with the test - we could not be dogmatic about what if anything the test revealed, simply because we did not know!

Our first validation study was to disconcert us slightly. We had decided to use, as our criterion, the percentage increase in salary over a given period: that was at least objective in the sense that it could be measured and it also provided some indication of the graduate's success within the company. We found a slight but significant negative correlation between test score and salary in a small pilot sample. This was not exactly what we had expected!

It is true that the results wait to be confirmed by a much larger study but it will not be surprising if the pilot study's results are confirmed. There is some evidence that a level of intelligence above a certain point (or in popular terms, too high an IQ) can be a handicap, sometimes, and especially in business. This may be a reflection on the type of test rather than on 'intelligence'.

Those who work with tests are used to surprises of the kind that we found in our pilot survey. There is a well known story of an Army test for drivers which turned out to be no good at all for drivers, but an excellent test for selecting women Army clerks! The point was that part of an Army driver's job was to fill in a very detailed log book and the test was particularly designed with an eye to that part of his job, which is why it was so appropriate for women Army clerks. What matters - as always - is what the test is supposed to measure and whether it really measures it or not, and that is the reason for validating it.

THE CLASSIC APPROACH

There is one last point. Testing got a big boost during the Second World War when people had to be trained quickly; tests helped to weed out the less able and so to lower training time. In peacetime, the speed of learning may not be so essential and so borderline cases can be accepted and these, if given proper training, can turn out very well. For example, in one study which we made of women 'teachers' - who are the junior supervisors who train newcomers in the art and skill of packing chocolates - we were able to carry out an almost classic 'controlled experiment'. What we did was to interview and test all those who applied for the job of a teacher. We then put our assessments on one side and proceeded to train two-thirds of those who had applied, but not to train the other third. But all who applied were then employed as teachers - whether recommended or not, trained or untrained - and their subsequent prowess was assessed. Fifty-seven per cent were rated as 'good' teachers, 43 per cent as 'poor'. But of those we had recommended for training 87 per cent turned out well. This demonstrated that systematic selection methods can pick a majority who are going to be successful and weed out those who are likely to be unsuccessful; but there is always a group in the middle who, if given good and proper training, can be turned from indifferent performers to successful ones. For 65 per cent of those we had not recommended turned out to be good teachers *after training* whereas only 16 per cent of those who were neither recommended nor trained were equally good. As Field Marshall Wavell once said, you cannot make a silk purse out of a sow's ear - but you can make a very serviceable leather one. In industry, perhaps, leather is better than silk!

HINTS ON USING TESTS

If you do use tests, do not be surprised if they sometimes produce unexpected results. What is essential, before even embarking on the use, is to make sure that you have someone on your staff who is properly qualified to give the tests, to score them and to interpret them. Equally you will need to make sure that you know what any test you intend to use purports to measure and if it actually does measure something measurable. Any figures of test results in other firms or in other industries will not, of course, absolve you from validating the test in your own organization. We have for many years allowed people to come and look at the sort of tests we have used; a few have even suggested that they might like to buy from us the tests which we have developed, standardized and validated. We have always refused, because we know only too well that these tests would have to be revalidated on their factory population, that this would take time and that they might not perhaps have the facilities to do it properly. Again, remember that tests should never be used in isolation. Very often, the full interpretation of a test score can only be given after an interview in which apparent contradictions or possible pointers have been examined. For example a high test score but low school or university achievement needs investigating. Equally, it will pay to consider the level of a candidate's interests, in the light of his test scores, or his choice of job or attainments in other spheres. Tests measure only some aspects of an individual: his ability or talents. It is the relation of those aspects to other facets that matters. Tests are but one part of a selection programme in which many other things have to be taken into account. Nor is a test score the end of the matter; as the example of the teachers show, it is only the beginning: if systematic training follows systematic selection then there is a greater likelihood of success in the long run.

3

Use of Tests in the Post Office Corporation

W. A. Furness

PSYCHOLOGICAL TESTS FOR POSTMEN?

This is a question which is frequently asked with not a little curiosity, and the affirmative answer met with some incredulity. Why this should be so, I am not sure, for the Post Office, a public corporation since 1969, has a tradition, stretching back many years into the days when it was a department of state, of written examinations being used to set the standards for entry to grades at all levels. Times and methods change, but the concept of assessing suitability for employment by interview supplemented by examinations and, increasingly, psychological tests has remained and been developed.

The Post Office employs more than 400 000 people, in four largely independent businesses: posts, telecommunications, data processing service and the National Giro banking service. All four demand large numbers of recruits with varying levels of qualifications and experience.

Some idea of the numbers can be gauged by looking at the 1974 recruitment figures given in Figure 3:1 for some of our larger grades of staff.

This by itself does not tell the whole story as vacancies for some grades are frequently heavily oversub-

Figure 3:1 Numbers recruited by the Post Office in various grades in 1974

Clerical grades (clerical officer and assistant)	5 235
Technical apprentices (trainee technician apprentice)	2 672
Telephonists	12 224
Postmen	19 572
Postal officers (recruited for Post Office counter work)	2 100

scribed. For example, in recruiting under 3000 technical apprentices in 1974, over 19 000 applications were dealt with. The Post Office is also a major recruiter of graduates; over 7000 applied in 1973 to fill 786 posts.

The areas of activity can be divided into the recruitment of managerial staff (predominantly graduates) and of those below managerial level (postmen, telephonists, clerical, technical and engineering staff, and data processing staff). The Corporation also recruits graduate engineers, scientists and computing and other specialists (80 in 1973).

The Civil Service Commission was responsible for all recruitment procedures until 1969 when this responsibility passed, in the case of graduate recruitment, to a newly established Post Office Appointments Centre. Recruitment of staff below managerial level continued to be undertaken locally, though with some central control over the procedures and methods adopted.

REASONS FOR USING TESTS

Many of the Post Office's selection procedures, particularly at the below-management level, have developed out of Civil Service examinations. In the course of time these have changed into objective tests, becoming at once wider in the area of coverage (including, for example, assessment of personality characteristics) and more specific in the area being tapped by any one measure.

One factor that has encouraged and assisted the development of modern testing practices is the high ratio of applicants to vacancies in some grades. For most grades interviewing ten applicants for every vacancy would be an uneconomic task; instead tests can be used as screening devices to reduce the number of promising applicants to a **man**ageable size. Tests are relatively cheap, and the cut-offs can be adjusted so as to accept only the number that can be processed comfortably. They have the virtue of being fair by setting the same standard for all.

The technical advantages of properly constructed tests are also of great importance to an organization that recruits in virtually every town of any size in the country for basically similar kinds of work. Particularly for below-management levels, tests are seen as providing some control over the standard of those recruited, by providing some objective information for local recruiters (who will be the employer) that enables any applicant to be assessed against a nationally determined minimum standard. This aspect of job-relatedness is important when the relative value of tests and educational qualifications as screening devices is considered. Tests can be validated and replaced or amended if necessary, in contrast to educational qualifications which are not designed as employers' selection tools. The Post Office, in common with many employers, uses educational qualifications as a very crude initial device. However, this merely defines the target population from which the most suitable will be selected eventually with the assistance of measures such as tests.

TESTS FOR SELECTION AT BELOW-MANAGEMENT LEVELS

At this level a great variety of tests is in use. They can broadly be categorized into five main groups:

1 Tests of clerical skills (e.g. checking and/or filing of verbal or numerical information).
2 Tests of numerical skills (i.e. requiring calculations of various kinds).
3 Tests of verbal ability (writing skills).
4 Tests of general intelligence (reasoning ability).
5 Tests for special aptitudes (e.g. mechanical aptitude, drawing ability, spatial sense).

For many grades the intention is to provide a test battery which combines elements of relevant educational attainments, specific aptitudes and various kinds of reasoning ability which may be important in the job applied for.

The criterion against which a test should be judged is whether or not it predicts to any extent successful performance at work. Within each of the five groups above there are tests at varying levels of difficulty covering different aspects of each skill. Tests of numerical skill for example, range from simple computation, where the emphasis is on speed and accuracy, to tests measuring the extent of mathematical knowledge. Tests also cover different aspects of skill with figures - for example, the ability to interpret the significance and trends of information presented in numerical form, or requiring the candidate to give a 'best-estimate' answer rather than work through a problem in detail. Some tests are available commercially; others (an increasing proportion) are developed internally for sole use by the Post Office. For selection for any grade, a suitable battery of tests must be assembled through careful investigation of the work to be done, the demands it makes on people who have to do it and, ideally, some validation evidence obtained on a group of staff who are currently doing the work.

The labels of tests and the labels given to jobs unfortunately do not always correspond: many tests of clerical aptitude contain a subtest in which the candidate has to check numerical and verbal material for errors, on the basis that many clerical jobs require this ability. We have noted, however, that this faculty - perceptual speed - can be found in many other jobs (e.g. telephonist, postman, punch card operator) and can form a useful addition to a test battery used for selection to jobs which may not have the word 'clerical' or any reference to clerical work in their job description. For this reason we now try to classify tests we use according to content and areas of measurement using labels which make no assumptions about the kinds of job or work for which they will be useful predictors.

TESTS FOR SELECTION AT MANAGERIAL LEVELS

Recruitment to managerial and professional posts is somewhat different. Since its inception the Appointments Centre has developed considerable expertise in 'extended interviews' using two-man teams who deal with a group of four to six candidates on any one day. One member of each team is a full-time assessor, a line manager, on secondment for two or three years and located in the Appointments Centre; the other is a middle or senior manager from one of the four Post Office businesses. The core of the procedure is two individual interviews, one with each assessor, with different areas covered by each. All assessors have been trained both in interviewing and in the interpretation of test results and other data. Tests come into the procedure at two stages, an initial test session acting as a screen to bring forward the most promising candidates to the second stage where they have interviews and further tests, which are used as additional sources of information to the assessors. In particular they will provide information in areas that may be difficult to tap during the interviews or in any other way. It is emphasized to candidates that tests are not used as pass-fail devices. The objective of the second stage is to make available as complete a picture as possible of each candidate covering both strengths and weaknesses, including areas where development may be needed. The assessors' task is not just to decide on selection or rejection; it is also to recommend placement into the most appropriate type of work, at one of two levels, and frequently to recommend geographical location. Work graded at the same level may differ quite considerably from one type of location to another so that candidates' abilities and aptitudes as well as their wishes are both relevant and important.

At this level assessors are predominantly looking for potential. Therefore, past educational attainments are unlikely to be directly relevant except for specialist/professional posts.

Important requirements are a willingness even as a non-technical manager to appreciate technical matters and some degree of numeracy, though not necessarily reflected in formal mathematical attainments. Candidates have to sit one or more tests of reasoning power to indicate their ability to continue to learn in a demanding managerial function. They also take tests of appropriate numerical skills and an exercise designed to find out how well they can set out in writing a particular point of view about a hypothetical case. Some will also take a test which approximates to a typical management problem (again with a quantitative flavour) which also allows scope for judgment and decision-making.

For specialist candidates there may be additional tests of attainment in the subjects pursued during their further education. Finally for the higher of the two graduate entry levels, there is a paper-and-pencil test of personality characteristics, the results of which are available to the assessor before his interview as an aid to him in planning the interview. Sometimes practical exercises are undertaken in a situation analogous to real life; for example, working as a member of a committee.

All of this implies a fairly busy day at the second stage. How does this mixture of tests, exercises and interviews go down with candidates? In fact it seems to be accepted remarkably well. One might suspect that making graduates take intelligence tests or engineers tests of engineering principles might cause problems of acceptability, but our experience indicates that this is not so. Indeed many graduates value objective tests as a counter to the 'subjectivity' of the interview and some who feel they have not given of their best in an interview say that tests allow them the opportunity to show what they really can do. Managers, even those from a quantitative discipline, can become among the most enthusiastic supporters of testing, once they appreciate the rigour and method which tests may bring to the 'subjective' process of selection.

TESTS FOR PROMOTION

The Corporation tries to recruit people who are expected to remain and make a career in the Post Office and seeks to select and develop senior management from its own staff, only rarely filling senior posts from outside. This has meant that considerable attention has been paid to devising open, fair and equitable promotion channels and procedures. In recent years new recruits have had rising expectations about opportunities for promotion. Coupled with this is a feeling that the traditional procedures, often based on a minimum length of satisfactory service prior to being called for interview before a three-man board, place too great a premium on 'time served' as a necessary qualification before promotion can be considered. These and certain organizational considerations have given rise to experiments which attempt to assess potential more directly by the inclusion of tests and exercises which measure qualities important in managerial functions, while at the same time placing less emphasis on job knowledge. The new procedures do not ignore current work performance but the overall focus is on enabling those who show promise at any level to be identified and moved or promoted to another kind of work as soon as they are ready for it.

CONCEPT OF THE ASSESSMENT CENTRE

The experimental procedures for deciding about promotion are like the 'extended interviews' described earlier. This kind of procedure comprises the major elements of what has come to be known as the 'assessment centre'. This approach was developed in the early 1940s by the War

Office Selection Boards (WOSBs), and later by the Civil Service (CISB); and in the United States notably at the American Telephone & Telegraph Company by Dr Douglas Bray.

The important characteristics of an assessment centre include individual interviews by one or more assessors, and the use of tests and other exercises previously shown to be related to important dimensions of managerial performance; for example communication skills, tolerance of work pressure, initiative or judgment.

Such procedures have begun to be incorporated experimentally in internal promotion systems by the Post Office, and tests of the paper-and-pencil kind described earlier and situational exercises such as the 'in basket' or committee exercise, for long accepted as suitable for open recruitment, are now showing themselves capable of providing useful information about potential to assist in promotion/development decisions.

CASE FOR INCLUDING TESTS AND OTHER EXERCISES IN PROMOTION PROCEDURES

In all Post Office promotion procedures, the written appraisal of performance plays an important part. Typically, in the absence of tests and other objective exercises, assessment of potential in areas that cannot adequately be examined during an interview is solely dependent upon the written appraisal.

All possible steps are taken to offset the problems arising from the varying standards of assessors and differences in the jobs. However, the use of suitably developed objective tests can do much towards improving what, with the best will in the world, will always be a less-than-perfect situation. Assessment centre techniques face the candidate with real-life 'business situations' directly related to performance at the next level up. They can also take account of current performance. As such they appear to be a better way of equalizing opportunities of promotion among candidates with dissimilar background and experience.

SOME CURRENT USES OF TESTS IN PROMOTION PROCEDURES

Interest and experimental work in the Post Office is currently focused on three areas:

1 Identifying at an early stage staff with management potential from among below-management levels.

2 Identifying staff with management potential from among specialist staff.
3 Identifying senior-level management potential from among junior or specialist management.

VALIDATION

Problems of Validation

The Post Office faces similar problems to those encountered by other organizations in selecting, defining and developing suitable criteria of work or training performance against which to measure the efficiency of tests and other selection procedures. Some of these problems are exacerbated by the size of the organization, while in some respects this factor can be a positive advantage.

On the debit side of the size factor is the fact that what is nominally the same kind of work can be undertaken in a variety of ways and thus can make different demands on job incumbents depending on the part of the organization or the location in the country. Thus, any attempt to validate selection tests for one grade must face up to the problem of obtaining information on work performance that (1) applies to all or even most members of the grade and (2) reflects accurately the performance of individuals on a common basis, uninfluenced by variations in how the work is organized.

To take one example, the job of dealing with complaints about the quality of the telephone service differs considerably in the kinds of demands it makes on employees. In some areas equipment is more modern and in greater supply than in others, so fewer complaints of breakdown and overloading may be reported. In addition part of the folklore of telephone service staff is that subscribers in some areas are more prone to complain than others, and this does not appear to be related to the quality of equipment in use. In this situation any hard data about number of complaints, time taken to rectify faults, or number of complaints taken to a higher level are invariably determined in part by variations which are not related to differences in individual performance by the staff concerned. This will obviously detract from their value as criteria against which selection tests can be evaluated.

The result is that we tend to rely perhaps too much on reports completed by higher-level staff, rather than more objective methods of assessment of performance. These reports may comprise a very structured series of ratings on various dimensions, or they may contain a 'pen-picture' or both.

At managerial level, assessment of performance raises difficulties for any organization. In particular for the Post Office, the current structure of many promotion and development systems makes objective data from the work field hard to come by or to use with confidence, except without a good deal of prior research. For example, reliance on fixed incremental salary scales, seniority lists and fixed hierarchies for progression, features which the Post Office retains from its days as a department of state, all tend to group entrants at any one level together, in terms of progression, so that only the very exceptional achieve promotion more quickly than the average. One can obtain some measure of differences in performance but, as the very exceptional are usually few in number, it can be difficult in some cases to obtain objective data which discriminate sufficiently between staff. However, changes are taking place which may result in the more able passing through the organization more quickly and this might improve the situation.

One major advantage of the large numbers of staff involved at all levels is that, unlike many validation studies particularly at the managerial level, insufficient numbers in samples studied is seldom a problem. In addition, because of the numbers involved, there is a reasonable chance of being able to subdivide the total population of job holders into subgroups according to age, sex, work location and function.

Despite the somewhat gloomy picture I may have painted, validation can be and is carried out within the limitations imposed by each particular situation. (We have, for example, given advice on the design of report forms to assist those completing them to achieve equal standards of assessment on relevant dimensions of performance.)

Validation at the managerial level

At the managerial level the relatively short existence of the Appointment Centre and the procedures it employs has meant that validation to date has principally consisted of special reports by supervisors one and two years after entry. In the near future it is hoped to start examining more objective data which should by now have accumulated in a reasonable quantity. We have felt it important that, wherever possible, reports should be seen as completely separate from the regular appraisals of staff, so that those completing them can do so frankly, in the knowledge that the assessment will not affect an individual's career progression in any way. We have insisted on this at the expense of some criticism of 'not another form' as it is essential to get some reasonable discrimination between individuals in the sample to make the exercise worthwhile.

As well as providing information on the quality of recruits generally, the dimensions represented on the form provide some information about the validity of individual parts of the selection procedure, including tests. Results inevitably range from the 'quite promising' to the 'frankly disappointing', though it is as well to remember that very high relationships are difficult to establish where the criteria are ratings, particularly when these are made by a large number of individuals. Also, for the management grades the sample available for study is a very highly selected group from the original field of applicants.

Figure 3:2 illustrates how far a reasoning test predicted a rating by supervisors who were unaware of the original test scores, two years after selection, for a group of 169 of the lower-level management entry. (The test grades on the lefthand side of the table refer to the Post Office system of norms — the higher the grade, the better the performance achieved on the test.)

Figure 3:2 Rating of 'intellectual qualities'

Grade on test	'Very good'	'Fully satisfactory'	'Only just satisfactory' or 'not satisfactory'
5-7	58%	40%	16%
4	24%	33%	42%
1-3	18%	27%	42%
	100%=66	100%=84	100%=19

The data collected only justified division of the performance measure into three groups. Even so there is a reasonable trend for those who obtained high marks on the test at selection to be rated better after two years of work than their lower-scoring colleagues. The problem of small numbers in the 'unsatisfactory' group is a limitation of the data available.

Another high-level test of reasoning power produced a correlation coefficient of 0.52 when related to a rating of 'overall suitability' for the work for a group of 48 of the higher-level management entrants ($p<0.05$). This and other evidence has helped to confirm the opinion that intellectual skills are important in higher-level management jobs. Tests of specific skills of various kinds have also been used as predictors of related aspects of work - in some cases with favourable results; in other cases not (for example, correlation coefficient of 0.68 for a test of interpretation of statistical data against a rating of numerical skills for 81 entrants but only 0.20 for a test of writing skills against a rating of writing ability for 67 entrants). When results are not encouraging in short-term (approximately one to three years) follow-up studies, it can sometimes be difficult to know what to make of them. Particularly with regard to management trainees, some skills may not be utilized to any extent in the early stages of a career. Alternatively, too early a display of some personality traits which may be important later on may not be fully appreciated by an organization when the individual is in a junior position. In either case a subjective judgment has to be made on whether it is worth persevering with a particular measure, after initially disappointing results, to see if it improves in the middle-to-longer term when there may be more opportunity for the attribute being measured to be displayed.

Validation at below-management levels
At the below-management levels, an additional source of information may be available on staff who take outside examinations. This is the case, for example, with technical apprentices who study for a range of City and Guilds qualifications. Results here can provide an objective measure of performance where the standard is the same throughout the country. Figure 3:3 indicates the relationship between the apprentice selection tests and three City and Guilds Intermediate Certificate examinations.

A final example illustrates the reservations expressed earlier about objective data. A series of tests is currently being introduced to select operators for punch-card and other computing equipment. On the face of it, this would seem the ideal situation for some objective data, for example, the number of keystrokes per hour on a card-punching machine. In practice, however, the variations from centre to centre between types of equipment, workloads and organization of work is so great that it has been virtually impossible to use this source of

Figure 3:3 Relationship between grade in an apprentice selection test and success in a public examination

Course: 'Maths for telecommunications(A)'

Grade on test	Pass	Fail	Percentage failing examination
6-7	183	6	3%
5	306	40	12%
4	169	23	12%
1-3	22	9	29%
	680	78	

Course: 'Telecommunications principles(A)'

Grade on test	Pass	Fail	Percentage failing examination
6-7	162	32	16%
5	276	79	22%
4	144	48	25%
1-3	18	10	36%
	600	169	

Course: 'Telephony and telegraphy (A)'

Grade on test	Pass	Fail	Percentage failing examination
6-7	181	11	6%
5	297	58	16%
4	159	30	16%
1-3	18	10	36%
	655	109	

data for validation. It was possible, however, to produce a correlation coefficient of 0.35 for 192 operators between test results and supervisor ratings.

Objective data become valuable where the content and organization of work to be done can be controlled - for example on training courses. In the real-life working situation, it is necessary to examine objective data closely to ensure that the assessment they provide of an individual's performance is not contaminated by other factors.

TESTS IN USE – SOME PRACTICAL CONSIDERATIONS

The tests and other exercises used by the Post Office are selected, developed, distributed and validated by a unit employing a small number of psychologists. I should like to discuss briefly some of the points to which the unit has found it necessary to pay attention in dealing with more than 400 local centres where tests are used but where there can be little direct supervision.

Training

Wherever tests are used in a number of different locations, attention must be given to training for all staff likely to be involved - whether they be administering and scoring the tests, or interpreting the results. Where the level of interpretation is fairly low, all three functions may be carried out by one person. For selection to management posts the administration and scoring of tests is kept separate from the interpretation of results which is carried out by the interviewers.

Regardless of the particular arrangements, all staff concerned with the new procedures require some training. In the three years since new selection tests for technical apprentices were introduced, the unit has trained over 300 of the engineering training staff (also responsible for selection) to administer the tests and to interpret the results. Also when preparing for a revised scheme for assessing suitability for promotion to junior engineering management, special courses were run for 48 test administrators and 72 assessors. Although training of this order places a considerable strain on professional resources, we have found that this is not the main problem. For tests to make as full a contribution as possible, the quality of administration and usage must be of a high order. A poor or slovenly administration which may involve candidates being inadequately prepared or time limits not being scrupulously observed can make a test useless. Similarly, mistakes in scoring or rash or unintelligent interpretation of the results by an interviewer can turn a perfectly valid test into a biased and unfair instrument. In our situation where it may be necessary to deal with up to 100 test administrators for any one battery such staff must come to a central location for training where close attention is paid to the content and quality of the training course. For many of the staff involved, test administration forms only a very small part of their work - perhaps less than two months in any one year.

Our call on their time therefore must compete with other work priorities. Therefore, we are particularly careful to make full use of training time.

Once training is completed and the procedure is in operation, we have found it advisable to maintain close contact with test centres and to encourage those using the tests to contact us over any points that may be worrying them. Some unforeseen problems always arise in the introduction of a new procedure and, if specialist advice cannot be obtained quickly, test centres will deal with them in their own way, thereby weakening the uniformity of the system. The central unit would not, however, provide on-the-spot interpretations of an individual's test results, particularly by telephone, since it can almost never be in full possession of all the facts relating to an application. The role of the central unit is strictly limited to providing tests and other means to assist management in reaching its decision.

Security arrangements

It has been found necessary to include in training some discussion of procedures to be adopted if tests and other confidential papers are to be kept securely and moved from one part of the country to another without threat of compromise. Commonsense is frequently the best guide, but much is gained if security procedures are stated rather than assumed. For example, when tests are not in use they must be locked up. They should always be double-wrapped when sent by post. When local centres return material to the unit in London, they send a separate notification so that, if a packet fails to arrive, a search can be started promptly.

Opinions differ on whether it is preferable for a test to be easily identifiable so that if it is lost then a finder can return it, or whether it should bear no marks of identification to minimize the risk of unauthorized use. We have aimed for a system whereby test papers contain no indications of what grade of staff they are used for, while at the same time indicating a point of return should they fall into unauthorized hands. The unit is also aiming for a system of separate question books and answer sheets. The question books can be kept at test centres, while only the answer sheets need to be moved.

It may be felt that the above arrangements are unnecessarily bureaucratic but one can only point to the possible serious consequences of even a minor loss. The considerable work involved in developing and validating a test can be entirely wasted if there were to be any suspicion that it might be available to some candidates in advance. The Post Office is particularly sensitive to issues of fairness in dealing with both staff and applicants for employment, and thus tends to be cautious in this respect.

Is one version of a test enough?
One problem that arises as tests are increasingly used in the Post Office is that there can be too few suitable tests to meet all purposes. For example the number of commercially available tests of high-level reasoning is limited. As a consequence these tend to be widely used by organizations recruiting from the same sectors of the population, e.g. graduates. Being a large organization we try to overcome this by developing our own tests.

Another reason for developing many of our own tests is that there are occasions when it is advantageous for more than one version of a test to be available. For example, one person may be due to take a test, part of an assessment procedure, which was used when he was selected. To ensure absolute fairness we aim to have available three or even more versions of an aptitude or ability test.

Standards of scoring
In order to ensure that high standards are maintained the unit monitors standards of scoring. A sample of used test papers is check-scored and if significant errors are found then the papers are returned to the local centre to be scored again. It is essential that this be done promptly otherwise it will be of only academic concern to the current batch of candidates. The necessity of achieving high standards in scoring is often underestimated. Once the scoring system has been learnt, it becomes a routine activity and there is a temptation to pass the work on to someone who may have had inadequate instruction, or for the trained individual to give insufficient attention to an apparently easy task. Experienced psychologists are themselves not immune from mistakes of this kind. The only solution is to check-score as high a percentage of papers as possible, with prompt referral where necessary.

Achieving acceptability of tests
One problem to be faced on introducing any procedure incorporating tests is that of overcoming the initial scepticism that may be felt by some about their value. In the majority of cases, such scepticism is often

rational and justifiable. After all the unit and its
psychologists are not themselves responsible for the final
decision. It is probably a mistake to devote too much
energy to dealing with this before recruiters have experience of using the tests, particularly as this may give
the impression of overselling the virtues of using tests.
In practical terms, when any test is first introduced,
regardless of prior validation, it is on trial until it
gains acceptance by those who have to use it. A good deal
of resistance can be overcome by proper presentation of
the tests and their purpose, particularly if one indicates how results can be interpreted in ways which provide
practical and useful information. However, our experience
has been that no matter how well tests are introduced full
confidence will not be achieved until the recruiting
officer has used them for some time.

In the early stages, those using tests frequently ask
for guidance on the interpretation of scores. We have
found that both psychologists and test developers tend to
underestimate this need. The test manuals for many commercially available tests tend to mention interpretation
only in passing. Thus we are moving towards the concept
of introducing a selection 'package', rather than just a
test, by including guidance on interpreting test scores,
together with typical profiles that might be encountered;
guidance notes on conducting an interview and interview
report forms which specifically refer to test results -
all to encourage users to view tests as a sound source of
information which can be used to supplement information
obtained in other ways.

Presentation of validation studies
The process of gaining acceptance for tests is hastened
by feeding back to users evidence of the usefulness of
tests. However, it is important that such information be
presented in a form which is meaningful to those for whom
it is intended. Validation findings, for example, are
frequently presented in the form of correlation coefficients, which may or may not be understood by those using
the tests. While I would deprecate any dressing-up of
results to claim more for a test than is justified, we
have found it useful to present results in a form which
highlights the practical contribution that even a test of
moderate validity can make to certain selection situations.

4

Use of Tests in United Biscuits

D. Wilson

PROCEDURE FOR TESTING DURING SELECTION

Two hours before the interviews at which a systems analyst will be selected by the management services manager, three candidates arrive and are shown into a quiet conference room. They are met by a personnel officer who tells them that they are going to take three psychological tests.
   He explains that the tests are part of the total selection procedure and that the results will be taken into account along with interview results and information on their application forms. One of the candidates indicates that he is anxious about taking psychological tests and asks if they can give any information of real value. The personnel officer explains that, like all methods used in selection, tests are not infallible and this is why the results of the tests are considered alongside interview and biographical data. He goes on to explain that the company has found the results of tests do bear a relation to successful work performance on the job and they help to reduce the number of occasions when candidates have found the work they have been asked to do not to their liking. The personnel officer then administers the tests and when they are completed asks if there are any questions. One

of the candidates refers to one particular item in the test which has caused some amusement, but generally speaking the candidates are much less anxious now than they were before they started. The candidates are told that they will not be informed of their individual test results just as they will not be informed of the detailed assessments that are made of them at the interview.

They will, of course, be told the result of the complete selection process. It is now two hours since the test programme started and after a short break the interview sequence begins.

While the interviews are taking place the tests are marked and interpreted and a report on each candidate produced in plain English. The personnel officer then visits the management services manager to discuss the test results and the interview findings. The test information is found to illuminate some parts of the interview and information gathered at the interview shows how certain aspects of personality indicated by the test are reflected in the persons' behaviour and life style. After full consideration, decisions are taken. The test results are sent to the central personnel department for future checks on the accuracy of predictions based on test and interview results. So far as individuals are concerned, test results are not reused beyond about two years.

GENERAL APPROACH OF THE COMPANY TO TESTING

United Biscuits has 25 000 employees at 15 major locations, and is a British company, with a turnover of about £250 million a year. As tests are now quite widely used, it is only possible (in the space available) to look at some examples rather than give a comprehensive survey of test usage. The main aim is to describe the practical benefits the company has gained through using tests rather than to enlarge on the theoretical implications of test usage. In particular, I shall show how the benefits were not always the ones that were expected!

The general approach which we have used is less than totally systematic, which is perhaps unavoidable in a large company but does have value in that it has encouraged line managers to use tests and to build up experience in their interpretation. We have preferred to encourage and train line managers to understand tests rather than to develop the mystique of the industrial psychologist. This approach has paid off handsomely in management attitudes to tests.

Because line managers understand, at least in general terms, how tests work they do not feel bamboozled nor do they feel held to ransom by technical specialists. Our approach has, if anything, led to over-enthusiasm of line managers and our problem, if we have one, has been to restrict the use of tests to situations where they can be shown to have value.

It has been our aim to have the operation of tests widely understood, by initially encouraging managers to use tests on themselves and on people they know well. We have made professional advice easily available as unobtrusively as possible and that has built up confidence in tests as an everyday technique of management. This approach has meant initially less-than-ideal control over test materials but where we have tried to impose strict regulations we have found resentment and even antagonism to the use of tests under such conditions. Managers want to understand, at least generally, the tools they are using. The main responsibility for making selection decisions lies with the line manager. He after all is going to employ the candidate so he must retain control of the selection process.

Tests are only one source of information which help him make a selection decision and results are therefore taken alongside results from interviews, performance reports, past job history, biography and so on. Although some companies find it possible to match individuals to job positions on the basis of statistical analysis this has not been our experience, particularly where development of the organization has meant that the best profile for a particular position changes from time to time. There seem to be very few jobs in United Biscuits where the ideal type of occupant remains constant year after year. We have therefore not found it practicable to produce descriptions of ideal occupants built up over time. Instead we have relied upon the manager's intuitive judgment in matching candidates to vacancies.

COMPANY POLICY

Tests were not introduced into company selection procedures in accordance with a general policy decision. Instead, they were introduced into individual locations over a period of time. After six or seven years it had become apparent that tests were sufficiently widespread in the company to warrant producing a company policy on their use, officially stating the attitude of the company to tests and establishing certain ethical procedures.

GRADUATE RECRUITMENT

Graduate recruitment is one of a number of special situations where past experience is not wholly relevant to future performance. It is necessary in these situations to understand the personality and motivation of the individual to judge how these will fit into the organization. It is economically very important to get the right answers because of the substantial investment which is put into graduate trainees. It can easily cost £1000 to recruit a graduate and it is unlikely that he will be making any substantial contribution to the organization in the first 12 months or so. Losing a graduate after a year's service can therefore cost £2000 to £3000. We recruit graduates in three stages.

The first stage is the preliminary interview at university lasting 20 to 30 minutes. The second is a one-day group selection procedure which is carried out on company premises and the third stage is an individual discussion with the employing line manager, usually carried out at the end of the one-day group selection procedure. Tests were introduced in the one-day selection procedure to give some depth and understanding of the candidates and to confirm assessments which have been made in other ways. We are now considering the possibility of using some sort of brief test at the initial university interview as a way of screening out obviously unsuitable candidates. The difficulty here is one of acceptability to the students rather than of technical feasibility.

A typical timetable for a one-day selection programme is given in Figure 4:1 from which it can be seen that tests occupy two hours out of a six-hour programme.

Figure 4:1 Stages in group selection programme for marketing trainees

1. Assessors' and candidates' introductions
2. Case study (60 minutes)
3. Company information (15 minutes)
4. Case presentation exercise (60 minutes)
5. Visit to offices (15 minutes)
6. Interview (30 minutes per candidate)
7. AH6 (60 minutes)
8. 16PF (40-60 minutes)
9. Peer rating (5 minutes)

This application of tests (basically personality assessment) was one of the first in the company and has continued to be one of the most important. Initially, tests were given and interpreted by an external consultant but eventually the company acquired sufficient ability amongst its personnel staff to do this internally. Because of the extent to which tests integrate into the overall selection procedure we have not found it practical to formally assess the validity of their contribution, and the value of tests lies in their ability to confirm and illuminate assessments which are made through other methods.

MANAGEMENT DEVELOPMENT

The use of tests in management development bears many similarities to their use in graduate recruitment.

The problem here is re-assessment and redirection of ability for the individual and stocktaking of management potential and ability for the company. In 1970 United Biscuits introduced assessment centres lasting three to five days as an aid to discovering the nature and extent of management ability within the company. A considerable side advantage has been that managers in mid-career have been encouraged to take some time to review their career and to discuss with a number of senior managers (not usually their immediate boss) the opportunities which might lie ahead of them, and their ability to cope with these opportunities. As part of this discussion, candidates at assessment centres have been provided with copies of the overall assessment which assessors have made of them. This feedback has then been used as a basis for a discussion on the manager's future career. One problem from the company point of view has been to equate standards across centres, especially when using different assessors.

Using tests and having some overlap between assessors has been found to help in ensuring consistency between centres. Some results from a series of company assessment centres are given in Figure 4:2.

When the high-rated and low-rated managers are compared on primary factors the former are seen to be more intelligent and more relaxed. To a lesser extent they tend to be more outgoing, more self-assured, more sensitive, more group oriented, 'less rule bound', less concerned over procedure and less shrewd. None of the differences were very great though the fact that there were observable differences on 12 of the 16 factors is noteworthy.

Figure 4:2 16PF and AH6 results for 50 middle managers attending company assessment centres (average age 35)

Test		Raw score means and standard deviations						
16PF		Low-rated managers (N=20)		Middle-rated managers (N=14)		High-rated managers (N=16)		
		$\overline{X}$	S.D	$\overline{X}$	S.D	$\overline{X}$	S.D	
A*	(20)**	10.9	3.7	10.5	2.4	12.4	3.3	
B	(13)	9.0	1.5	10.3	1.4	10.6	1.4	
C	(26)	16.7	3.5	18.9	3.0	18.1	3.2	
E	(26)	14.8	5.9	14.2	4.8	16.1	3.6	
F	(26)	13.1	3.0	13.7	4.1	15.4	4.6	
G	(20)	14.9	3.3	13.7	4.4	11.6	3.7	
H	(26)	16.2	5.2	15.4	4.1	16.6	5.7	
I	(20)	7.3	3.7	11.1	3.0	8.6	3.9	
L	(20)	5.9	3.5	7.1	2.8	6.9	3.3	
M	(26)	15.2	3.3	15.3	3.6	16.6	3.6	
N	(20)	9.9	3.2	9.3	3.3	8.3	3.3	
O	(26)	7.5	4.6	6.9	3.3	7.1	3.3	
Q1	(20)	10.5	3.3	10.4	3.0	11.7	2.8	
Q2	(20)	10.8	3.2	10.8	4.2	9.4	2.8	
Q3	(20)	15.0	3.3	13.7	2.2	12.5	2.8	
Q4	(26)	11.1	5.6	9.4	3.0	8.2	4.5	
AH6	PT1	14.4	3.6	18.1	4.4	19.5	3.6	
	PT2	13.6	4.2	14.7	3.5	18.5	4.5	
	Total	28.0	7.1	32.8	6.7	38.1	6.7	

* See Appendix 2 for description of factors
**Maximum possible score on trait

We found that providing results in numerical form was not very helpful. Instead we now produce a written report on each candidate which is a composite of the standard factor descriptions given by Cattell. Although this tends to look rather stilted it does have the advantage of being relatively objective and does not allow the tester's personal knowledge of the candidate to influence his report. Although used in preparing the report, test results obtained as part of the assessment centre data do not go on a manager's file; their use is restricted entirely to the preparation of the final report.

A typical test report follows.

Report on a manager prepared from the results of a 16PF test

He is socially outgoing, uninhibited and good at making and maintaining interpersonal contacts.

He tends to be one whose life is generally satisfying and is able to achieve those things that seem to him to be important. He may, however, lack sustained motivation for difficult tasks.

He tends to be aggressive, independent, daring and incisive person. He will of choice seek situations where such behaviour is at least tolerated and possibly rewarded. He is likely to exhibit considerable initiative.

He is likely to be a successful unofficial leader in a smallish group.

He has a high level of original creativity and will offer novel different contributions.

He showed a well-developed disposition for analytical critical thinking.

He has a strong inner drive to succeed. He will want to set and achieve objectives and goals. He needs to be told how much he is doing and is unhappy with long periods without guidance. He tends to set what for him are realistic rather than ideal goals.

Tends to be sedate, relaxed, composed and satisfied (not frustrated). In some situations, his over-satisfaction can lead to laziness and low performance, in the sense that low motivation produces little trial and error.

Tends to be cheerful, active, talkative, frank, expressive, effervescent, carefree. He is frequently chosen as an elected leader. He may be impulsive and mercurial.

Tends to be interested in intellectual matters and has doubts on fundamental issues. He is sceptical and inquiring regarding ideas, either old or new. He tends to be more well informed, less inclined to moralize, more inclined to experiment in life generally, and more tolerant of inconvenience and change.

Assertive, self-assured and independent-minded. He tends to be austere, a law to himself, hostile or extrapunitive, authoritarian (managing others) and disregards authority.

Tends to be emotionally mature, stable, realistic about life, unruffled, possessing ego strength, better able to maintain solid group morale. Sometimes he may be a person making a resigned adjustment to unsolved emotional problems.

Is sociable, bold, ready to try new things, spontaneous, and abundant in emotional response. His 'thick-skinnedness' enable him to face wear and tear in dealing with people and gruelling emotional situations, without fatigue. However, he can be careless of detail, ignore danger signals, and consume much time talking. He tends to be 'pushy' and actively interested in the opposite sex.

Tends to be unsteady in purpose. He is often casual and lacking in effort for group undertakings and cultural demands. His freedom from group influence may lead to anti-social acts, but at times makes him more effective, while his refusal to be bound by rules causes him to have less somatic upset from stress.

Final report on the same manager at an assessment centre

A very pleasant and initially reserved person who, if not for his hair colour, would not quickly be noticed in a group. However, once seen in a working group he soon makes his presence felt. He is a knowledgeable young man with considerable imagination and vision.

Although very obviously intelligent he lacks some experience because of his age and shows some immaturity.

Although he can think clearly and forwardly, he likes to stir up the thinking of others and enjoys being provocative. He shows courage in putting forward his views, some of which are off-beat and illustrate his characteristics of imagination and vision. He can move freely across a wide range of roles covering action and directing. He does, however, need to work in a stimulating environment, otherwise he tends not to contribute as much as could be expected. When working on mundane or routine matters, he tends to lose interest and show boredom.

He is full of personal confidence which enables him to take on other subjects and is not excitable or irrational in his behaviour.

His creative thinking comes out in his peer assessment reports which identify an ability to know and understand people. He has not been as successful as might have been expected in getting others to agree with his point of view. He needs more experience in dealing with this problem and was at times disheartened by his own failure in this direction.

He would seem to be suitable for a position requiring forward, imaginative and new thinking. His manner is a polite one and he should be an easy person to work with.

An ideal marketing man, and for long-term planning, but tends to be disinterested with routine.

His self-assessment indicates that he is aware of some of his shortcomings.

These reports stress differences between candidates at a particular centre rather than relating each candidate to the population at large. They thus accentuate the differences between candidates and make each individual's personality and abilities clearer. We also compare the means and distributions between centres to make sure each group of managers is a typical sample of the whole. The assessors on company management centres are usually at director level. These managers initially expressed great scepticism about the use of tests and it was possible to introduce them only in parallel with the other procedures.

Their curiosity was aroused, however, when they saw final reports and this led them to ask to do the tests themselves. Each director who took the test received a written report which he informally discussed with his colleagues (usually with his wife as well!) and these discussions led to a realization that tests were a reasonably effective way of obtaining a report on a man's personality quickly and easily and that they were not sinister devices. The acceptance of tests by directors was a major step forward in the introduction of tests to the company.

SUPERVISORY SELECTION AND DEVELOPMENT FROM WITHIN THE COMPANY

This is an account of a particularly opportune set of circumstances which allowed a comprehensive study of supervisors to be made. The initial briefing for this exercise came from one of the production directors who had experienced the use of tests at the assessment centres previously described. He asked that the abilities and nature of present supervisors be studied as a preliminary step in a programme intended to raise the level of supervisor performance. In addition he wanted to see if there were differences between groups of supervisors at different locations within his responsibility.

The study, carried out in five factories, involved about 60 supervisors (mainly female) at first-line level. In each of the factories it was stressed that individual results would not be available to local managers and that the objective was a factory result. Supervisors were asked to complete the 16PF and AH4 tests. They also completed three questionnaires: job satisfaction, personal achievement climate and achievement motivation.
In addition we asked factory managers to rank the job performance of each supervisor and the peer groups of supervisors also ranked each other. We were thus able to compare test results with 'success' as judged by the supervisor's boss and separately by his peers.

The Sten scores, primary factors and second-order factors are given in Figure 4:3. The scores which deviate more than 2 points from the mean of 5.5 are underlined. Inspection of the latter shows that in most instances when the difference is not ±2 points the general direction is the same — for example, in locations A, B and E the supervisors are definitely tough-minded while in locations

Figure 4:3 Mean Sten scores on primary and second-order factors on 16PF and AH4 scores for first-line supervisors in five factories

The factors are described in Appendix 2

	A	B	C	D	E
A	5	6	7	5	4
B	6	5	4	7	7
C	6	6	4	6	6
E	6	6	4	6	8
F	6	6	6	4	5
G	4	7	7	7	5
H	7	6	7	5	7
I	3	3	5	4	2
L	8	7	7	6	7
M	6	5	6	4	7
N	5	5	6	6	5
O	5	4	6	4	4
Q1	8	8	7	8	7
Q2	6	5	6	7	6
Q3	8	8	6	7	6
Q4	4	3	5	5	4
Extraversion	6.2	6.5	6.5	5.1	6.0
Anxiety	4.8	3.9	6.0	4.7	3.8
Tough poise	8.4	7.7	6.4	6.5	8.5
Independence	7.5	8.1	6.0	6.8	8.3
Leadership	7.2	8.1	6.3	7.2	7.2
Creativity	6.3	8.7	8.1	7.1	7.1
AH4 Part 1	B*	C	C	E	B
AH4 Part 2	C	C	B	E	C
AH4 Total	B	C	B	E	C

*A and E extreme 10 per cent
C   middle 40 per cent
B and D 20 per cent either side of C

C and D the tendency is less strong. This suggests that while some differences occur the overall pattern of supervisor personality in each location is not vastly different.

Inspection of Figure 4:4 clearly shows that supervisors ranked as 'good' by peers and bosses in some cases have similar personality attributes but in others have very different attributes. Also, although the supervisor personality pattern was rather similar in all locations the attributes that correlate with effectiveness are different.

Figure 4:4 Correlation between peer and boss assessments of success and personal characteristics of supervisors in five factories

Factor	A Peers	A Boss	B Peers	B Boss	C Peers	C Boss	D Peers	D Boss	E Peers	E Boss
Intelligent (AH4)			-0.67		0.75	0.61	0.48	0.40		
Outgoing					0.41	0.81				
Intelligent			-0.67							
Maturity		0.55				0.57	0.41		0.42	
Assertiveness	0.65	-0.52	-0.56	-0.50			0.61	0.77	0.56	
Cheerfulness							0.51	0.56		
Conscientious-ness		-0.52								
Socially bold					-0.47		0.47			
Tough-minded										
Realistic		0.46			0.49				0.40	
Trusting		0.63				0.40				
Imaginative			0.54		-0.47				0.43	
Shrewd	-0.62		0.76	0.56						
Self-assured									0.70	0.49
Experimentally minded		0.48		-0.67		-0.42	0.68	0.59		
Group-oriented				0.60					0.63	
Self-controlled		0.46	-0.50	0.67				0.54	0.54	
Relaxed		0.56	0.41						0.45	

In factory E, for example, eight of the basic factors correlated with the peer assessment. The person seen by the peers as a good supervisor appeared to be mature, cheerful, tough-minded, imaginative, self-assured, group-oriented and self-controlled. The only characteristic to correlate with the boss assessment was self-assurance.

In factory A an almost complete reversal is found; only three personality traits correlate with the peer assessment, while seven correlate with the boss assessment.

Further inspection of the table shows that different attributes seem to have predominated in the different locations. In three locations assertiveness was related positively to rating of success while in a fourth it related negatively and in the fifth it did not relate at all.

When we examined the ratings put in by both peers and bosses we found that there was in fact considerable agreement about who the successful individuals were. What was happening was that peers and bosses were looking at different aspects of the supervisor's personality - which is to be expected as each has a different set of expectations of the man.

At both factories C and E it was recommended that 16PF and AH4 be introduced into the selection procedure for future supervisors - but with slightly different aims for the AH4. At factory E there was clearly some advantage in getting future supervisors with AH4 scores towards or above the top end of the raw score ranges of the present staff (i.e. 31-51) as in this span scores seem to relate to performance. At factory C, however, the range was 58-117 and here there seemed to be little relation between scores and performance. The advice here was to select new supervisors who fell into the existing range and to question if we were really offering full opportunity to this obviously very able group.

On the 16PF the added detail given to the personal specification by examining peer requirements will lead, we hope, to selecting supervisors who can 'fit in' more easily and naturally than would be the case if only 'boss specification' was used. This is in line with our company policy of involving peers in the selection process wherever this is possible.

OTHER USES OF TESTS

In addition to the three areas already covered, tests are now widely used in the selection from salesmen of first-line managers and in the recruitment of production trainees, clerical trainees, engineering apprentices and computer staff. In addition, tests have been used in several one-off applications. For example, the selection of an in-company supermarket manager and the selection from shopfloor employees of trainees to undertake a two-year technical training programme. Generally speaking we use tests in a descriptive rather than statistical way although we usually do some simple statistical analysis as backup. It can be seen that we have not used tests alone but always in conjunction with other information.

We are in the preliminary stages of considering whether tests might be useful in screening situations, where there are a large number of applicants whom it is not possible to interview, for example, in the recruitment of graduates salesmen and operatives. All applicants would take a screening test and only those reaching an appropriate level would be interviewed. This would mean that we could spend longer on the selection of screened applicants but, as a counter to that, there is some anxiety that screened-out applicants who have not had a chance to be interviewed would see the company as 'inhuman' and that this might damage our long-term image, particularly at universities.

ADDITIONAL BENEFITS FROM THE USE OF TESTS

Tests have usually been introduced by the training or personnel function as an aid to selection or allocation decisions alongside existing methods. As confidence has built up and as it has been seen that the tests are more efficient or more reliable at giving the information that was given by the traditional methods they have become incorporated into the system.

I mentioned earlier that the use of tests produces some benefits which were not expected. One of these is that tests provide a focus of attention for judgments about people; the experience of being in discussions where test results and interview data have been compared appears to have improved the quality of interviewing and the care with which material from interviews is interpreted. Exercises linking test results to job performance have led to much better understanding of the real personal requirements for a job and have tended to be an effective argument against the very narrow definition of the ideal person to do a job which many managers have. We have regarded this as a healthy experience as it means we can be less restrictive in recruitment and have a wider range of people

in the company instead of a narrow company stereotype.
The use of tests at assessment centres has generated widely
accepted descriptions of people which are used and understood throughout the whole company. This has added to the
value of job-based assessments which were understood only
in a particular specialist area; for example, a production
man's abilities and personality can now be described by
the production director to the marketing director in a
common language which both understand.

This has facilitated cross-functional job transfers and
has laid the groundwork for much more effective utilization
of people's abilities. Because of the very natural suspicions which people have about tests, the company has been
forced to review the degree of openness in selection situations. This is gradually leading to counselling becoming
a normal follow-up to internal selection situations. Although we would very much like to provide feedback to
external applicants, it is not practicable at the moment
because of the time it takes.

INTRODUCTION OF TESTS

The first applications of tests were at junior level. In
fact the very first application seems to have been for
selecting biscuit packers to whom tests of manual dexterity
were given. The next application seems to have been with
graduates, then with managers and then the use of tests
mushroomed into the present position. There was initially
considerable antagonism towards tests at board level until
some directors took the tests at assessment centres and
became 'converted'. We found that individual objections
or refusals to taking tests have been very rare and where
they have arisen it has usually been possible to reassure
the applicant by explaining what the test is trying to do
and more particularly how the results will be used. The
one area that we have had difficulty with internally was
with computer staff who were mainly graduates and who were
suspicious that 'secret files' were being built up on them.

To deal with this we said that full feedback of test
results (but not just scores) would be given to individuals
and as a result of this the difficulties seem largely to
have vanished. We encourage, however, a healthy scepticism
about tests and discourage both those who take tests and
those who use them from a blasé acceptance of the results.
Tests may sometimes give a wrong impression. Even the most
basic test has to be treated with care and the results
interpreted in the light of the whole person to whom they

refer. As an example I should like to quote a factory employee who obtained a very low score on the AH4 test when applying for a position as a trainee technical adviser. The test evidence was clearly that he would not be able to cope with the course and would have difficulty in dealing with the intellectual requirements of the job. However, the man was very highly motivated and because of this was able to meet the requirements of the course and the job through sheer sustained persistence. The results he achieved on the training couse were entirely satisfactory and he is now a highly valued member of the technical adviser team. If only the test results had been taken into account, we would have lost a very valuable man.

In keeping with our policy of not building up any great mystique about tests we have allowed regional personnel staff to choose and use tests of their choice. The central personnel department has been very concerned, however, to provide professional supervision in the use of tests, particularly through the training of test administrators. All materials are ordered and stocked centrally so as to keep a check on the use of tests and to ensure they are not misused. In addition the central personnel department carries out validation exercises and assesses the value of new tests for special purposes.

For normal usage we find 5 tests satisfactory, although with the increasing number of special applications this number may increase. By far the most frequently used test is the 16PF where we use the anglicized 1967-8 version. Normally form A alone is used but in special circumstances we use form B and rarely form C or D.* We have a simple computer program for computing second-order factors and criterion results and have recently extended this to provide a full plain-English report. Using this program it is possible to obtain from the computer a descriptive report which can be given direct to a trained line manager and removes the chore of calculation entirely from the testers.

The next most frequently used tests are Alice Heim's AH4 and AH6. AH4 generally has sufficient range but we use AH6 for graduates, specialists and some management cate-

*Although it is more usual for commercial and industrial companies to use form C and form D, United Biscuits, which had a psychologist, began with form A. Since the manuscript was prepared, United Biscuits has increased the use of form C for applicants with less formal education than that usually found among managers and salesmen. (Editor.)

gories. We have found that for senior managers AH6 has fairly low acceptability and is regarded as a glorified 11+ exam. Although it is measuring a rather different ability, we are now trying to discover whether the Watson Glaser Critical Thinking Appraisal would be an acceptable substitute.

CONCLUSIONS

The position today, 1975, is that we have a fairly widespread acceptance of tests in the company. Our aim for the future is to improve our knowledge of the validity of the tests we are using and to provide interpretations which are more meaningful to line managers. We also aim to do this very quickly by using computer analysis. We now have one trained tester per major site and we shall increase as time goes by. We have established links with the Medical Research Council's Social and Applied Psychology Unit at Sheffield and have been working with them on various new tests to measure aspects of achievement motivation. In addition we have established links with the IARC who are working with us in developing professional skill in using tests. They have assisted by running internal courses for people concerned in administering tests and interpreting test results.
   We are at present working towards using personality tests more effectively in the recruitment of computer staff (although the NIIP report in this area would seem to offer little encouragement!).
   Having been doing concurrent validity studies for some time, we are just coming up to the stage where tests have been in use for long enough to carry out some predictive validity studies.
   Perhaps the biggest programme facing us is to develop procedures for using ability tests with immigrants. Because of the wide variety in background and language, conventional approaches to the development of norms seem inappropriate, and a much more thoroughly individualistic approach seems to be necessary. It would seem that this is an area where some academically sponsored research might be appropriate.

5

Graduate Selection

C. C. P. Ingleton

This chapter describes the progress of a research project into the use of psychological tests in the selection of graduates for an oil-marketing organization in the UK.

During a five-year period, in which the market for attracting top-class graduate recruits into industry has become very competitive, the company concerned has been administering a battery of tests to the majority of its 'second interviewees'. In total, 428 graduates were tested during these five years.

As with most large organizations, the company policy is to recruit 'the cream' of university graduates interested in a career in industry. In the words of a senior personnel manager in the company, their initial policy when considering the introduction of tests was 'to obtain the very best material (i.e. graduates) available for the organization; to do this, any innovation must raise the standards of both the candidates and their final selection'. In the document from which this quotation was taken, a great deal of effort was spent on outlining the organization's concern for a soundly based graduate selection procedure. It was recognized from the outset that the procedure should be acceptable to applicants as well as being as valid as current knowledge could make it.

With hindsight the most important point made was the

statement that 'The advantages of testing, and indeed the advantage of having a consultant psychologist, increase as the years pass. In many respects year one is an experimental model, from which will be built a better and improved system.' This policy document was prepared a full seven years before the present attempt at summarizing progress. In fact, as I hope to establish below, it was not until the fourth or fifth years of the research that the psychological test results themselves could be given anything but a minor weighting in the selection decisions. Even now, they are treated with caution by the 'consultant psychologist' involved. However, now in their fifth year of use, the test results are seen to be promising, especially in accurately indicating the final outcome of most candidates' applications to the research team.

This history of the research thus dates from the policy document mentioned, which was prepared in late 1967. The following year some 90 applicants were tested. A team of outside consultants administered a battery of three tests; however, the company found that the test results were inappropriate. The main problem was thought to be the lack of relevant test norms against which to evaluate test findings. Two of the tests in the battery used were from the USA, without relevant UK norms. There was also evidence that applicants at that time objected to the obvious 'Americanization' of the selection procedure. Accordingly one of the company's own psychologists assembled a battery of four paper-and-pencil tests (described in Figure 5:1) which were thought to be more appropriate to their needs. These were administered to groups of up to twelve applicants.

Figure 5:1 Initial test battery

		Timing
1	Raven's Progressive Matrices	60 minutes
2	ACER Speed and Accuracy Test	17 minutes
3	Thurstone Interest Inventory	25 minutes
4	Cattell Sixteen PF Questionnaire	50 minutes

The main value of these tests to the company was the fact that over 500 company personnel had taken part in a research project that year, to which the same tests had been administered (Ingleton 1972). The only exception was the Raven's Progressive Matrices, a test developed in the UK for which extensive UK norms were available. Even so, the tests were used with great caution in that year. No test results were provided to selectors; the tests were administered to candidates and then locked away to be used for research purposes only in a subsequent follow-up and for the provision of 'graduate' norms for use in the following year's graduate testing programme.

For the last four years the company has used a summary of the test results as a part of the graduate selection procedure, becoming more confident in their meaning (and thus increasing the 'weight' which selectors attached to them) as the years progressed. However, as Guion (1965) points out 'Tests are simply part of the process. They can be a big help when the final personnel decision is reached, but they do not make that decision.'

SELECTION PROCEDURE

The selection procedure is very similar to the pattern developed by most of the large companies on the graduate 'milk round'. Graduates are put in touch with the organization usually through their university careers and appointments officer. Having completed the company application form, they are interviewed on campus by a senior member of the organization who assesses their suitability for a second interview. Those who appear for this final stage in the procedure spend a day at the company head office, during which time they are given the opportunity to find out more about the company, and are in turn assessed for their suitability.

As well as being introduced to previously successful graduate applicants, to find out at first hand about the company, applicants complete a battery of tests, and are given a panel interview. Figure 5:2 outlines the sort of timetable which has been adopted over the last two years.

CURRENT TESTING PROCEDURE

Undoubtedly, the test about which most validation information exists is Cattell's 16PF (Cattell *et al.* 1970). In addition to an original sample of 563 company personnel, 43 middle managers and 140 other company personnel have completed this test (see Chapter 6). Also, 428 graduate applicants have provided test scores here, of which around 20 per cent finally joined the company in over 10 different types of jobs. Currently, most of the research is being devoted to the predictive validity of the 16PF; impressions gained from initial findings are the main concern of this chapter.

Figure 5:2 Typical applicant's timetable for second interview

Evening	-	Arrive in hotel	Dinner with recent graduate entrants
Morning	-	09 30	Complete Cattell 16PF
		10 15-10 30	Coffee
		10 30-11 30	AH6 test
		11 30-12 30	Test of quantitative aptitude
		Lunch	
		14 00	Panel interview with appropriate line and personnel managers who have a summary of test scores (but *not* the scores themselves
		15 00	Depart

Of the other tests used, the original battery was extensively modified as a result of the early experience. AH6 replaced Raven's Progressive Matrices, since it provides three scores: on spatial, verbal and numerical reasoning. Alice Heim also demonstrated a high correlation between scores on the Raven's and the spatial scale of the AH6 (Heim *et al*. 1970). The test of quantitative reasoning was adopted initially because of its high 'face' validity for many of the jobs for which the company required graduates. This measures logical inference, computational reasoning and the ability to interpret graphically presented data.

PROBLEMS ENCOUNTERED

The company policy is to use the most senior line manager involved in any appointment along with a senior personnel manager and a third line manager, in a panel interview. The main constraint on time is thus the availability of these senior people.

Interviews normally take place over a three-week period during the university Easter vacation with the tests being administered by the psychologist, normally to groups of between four and twelve graduates.

The main problems encountered seem to be in:

1 Preparing a report on the test scores in a format helpful to the interviewing panel.

2 Writing it between 12 30 (when applicants leave) and 14 00. (when the first interview begins).
3 Gaining the confidence of some of the brightest of university undergraduates who are healthily sceptical of the use of psychological tests.

The first difficulty is overcome by attempting to involve interviewing managers in the planning of any reporting procedure some months before the graduates are interviewed. A survey of their reactions to the use of tests is made each year (see the section on 'Reaction of line managers to tests'). Their comments about the aspects of the test reports that they find useful are taken into account when designing the current report form (which has been slightly modified in each year of operation).
 The second difficulty is overcome (barely) by the use of a computer program, written for the purpose by the company staff, to produce several of the 'second-order' scores from the 16PFQ. This is run virtually on-line twice a day: at 12 00 for the morning test session, and at 17 00 for the afternoon test session.
 The last problem is usually overcome by the use of a carefully worded 'test patter'. In addition, applicants are encouraged to ask any question they wish to about the origins of the testing, what the tests purport to measure, and how they are used by the selectors. The fact that there are two types of test is explained to them: a test of 'typical' performance (the 16PF), which samples their typical type of reaction to problems, and two tests of 'optimum' performance (see Cronbach 1973). Although it is possible to 'fake' the personality test this eventuality is discussed with the applicants, and it is stressed that the norms used were collected primarily as a research exercise. Thus they might well 'fake' themselves the profile of a job for which they are not suited. (However, there is tentative evidence that a certain amount of 'motivational distortion' is taking place, with the possibility of deliberate 'faking' suspected in a few of the applicants - see below.)
 This test is not timed but applicants tend to take between 30 and 45 minutes to complete it, and are invited to join the tester afterwards at coffee in a separate corner of the testing room. Their fears, usually about the unreal nature of the choices they have made to the questions, and the 'forced choice' nature of the questions, are normally brought out at this time. Coffee is extended until all applicants have finished the test and had time

to relax for a few minutes. The tests are then resumed;
with the two, timed, tests of optimum performance.

In general terms none of the applicants over the past
five years has refused to take the tests, although some
have expressed reservations about their use.

REACTION OF LINE MANAGERS TO TESTS

In 1974, ten senior line managers who sit on the three-
man selection panels (alongside one of their assistants
and the personnel manager) were individually interviewed
about their attitudes to the selection of graduates. A
semi-structured interview was used; the first question
concerned their experience of tests.

Four of the managers remembered that test reports had
been available to selectors at interviews the previous
year. One did not look at the test report, preferring to
leave it to the personnel manager; the other three did
consult the test reports, and were able to recount their
reaction to them. The general pattern seemed to be as
follows. If the test report coincides with the manager's
own judgment, the test is good. If the test report is at
variance with the manager's own view, the test is wrong
and should be ignored.

A fifth manager, although not using test reports, did
recall that his opening question in an interview would
usually be of the form, 'How did you get on in our tests;
did the psychologist make you work hard?' Here, the
testing procedure was presumably viewed as another hurdle
over which applicants had to jump.

Subsequent questions concerned managers' perceived
needs when selecting graduates. Despite their apparent
lack of interest in the value which tests might be in
assessing an individual, the managers were all aware of
the need to assess individuals with more accuracy than a
superficial chat might achieve. As a result of this
survey, far more care is being taken in presenting test
report data in a form which managers find useful, and can
interpret. Also, more effort is being put into increasing managers' awareness of the relationships between
test scores and job behaviour, and the limitations to
what can be achieved by the use of tests.

REACTION OF GRADUATES TO TESTS

Two surveys have been carried out in this area, one in
1970 and one in 1974. A similar questionnaire was used

in both surveys and, although no specific questions about the applicants' reactions to tests were included, two of the 'open' questions yielded comments about the tests. These were:

1 How far did the overall selection procedure enable you to present a full and accurate picture of your abilities?
2 What changes could be made to the procedure to make it as fair as possible to graduate applicants?

The numbers dealt with were small, of the 91 people surveyed in 1970, 37 replied (all within 10 days of being contacted) of whom 25 had been offered jobs and 12 had been rejected.

In 1974, only the graduates who had been offered jobs and had turned down the offer (18) were contacted. Of these 15 replied, of whom nine had completed the test procedure described in this chapter.

In the 1970 survey, the contents of the replies to the first question differed between those who had been offered jobs and those who had not. Only one of those offered a job thought that the procedure had not given him sufficient scope to display his abilities; his comment was, 'The interview could have been longer.' On the other hand, 10 of the 12 people rejected felt they had had a raw deal.

This finding as in line with Anderson's work (reported in Webster 1964) which makes up part of the 'McGill studies' on interviewing. This suggests that, where a decision is taken early on in an interview to reject an applicant, this will affect the amount of discomfort expressed by the applicant.

Of the 13 rejected applicants who replied, 11 commented unfavourably about the procedure, seven commented unfavourably about the interview, and three of these also commented unfavourably about the tests. Comments relating to tests were 'The interview was too short. Too high a proportion of the time was taken up with tests.' 'I thought the length of time (3 hours) conducting written tests was out of all proportion to their value and out of proportion to the length of the final interview (45 minutes).' 'No selection procedure can provide a fair opportunity to applicants. At the moment there is no satisfactory alternative to the use of interviews and tests.'

Of the 24 who were offered jobs, 23 thought the procedure was fair overall, although four commented unfavourably on the tests, as follows,'Some more relevant test would have been useful, e.g. on the ability of the student to apply the theory he has gained.' 'I was able to give a fair picture, but the written tests were far too long and boring.' 'I feel that the interview, personality and interest tests gave me adequate opportunity to present my personality. The intelligence tests lost importance in consequence.' 'I feel that perhaps a longer time could have been spent on the interview and less on the tests.'

In the 1974 survey, all nine respondents had been offered jobs, but had declined. Four of them felt that the procedure was fair. Of the other five, two commented unfavourably on the tests. Their comments were, 'No test really went into depth. Interviews are not fair as they usually favour the more articulate anyway.' 'I personally question the validity of psychological testing in this type of personnel selection. I found being interviewed by a panel of four made the presentation of a coherent picture difficult.'

The second relevant question concerned the changes graduates would like to see made in the procedure. In the 1970 survey, again, the types of suggestion tended to differ between those offered jobs and those rejected. Comments about faults in the procedure mainly came from the 'reject' group (nine in all), whereas a mixture of positive and negative suggestions came from the 'offer' group (four positive, eight negative). Overall, seven of the negative comments were about tests. Some respondents were critical of the test administration, rather than test content. For example, 'Do not give five tests in rapid succession to an applicant who has just spent five hours or more on a train.' Other respondents were critical of the 16PF test, 'In the personality test, some of the alternatives were not really alternatives.' 'I thought the personality test was farcical, at least, many of the questions were.'

The positive suggestions mostly advocated the use of different tests, for instance, 'Perhaps some sort of test could be devised that is specifically related to the type of work one would be doing' or 'Use some kind of general knowledge test.' Only one individual advocated extending the testing procedure, 'Include some objective form of assessment at the initial interview stage.'

In the 1974 survey, three comments were made about changing the testing procedure. Two of these were, 'I'm not convinced that the use of your psychological tests is any benefit.' 'If you want to use tests, use one not written against the clock, where the quality of answer counts.' 'Taking the same test in several firms may *not* affect your scores, but it makes you wonder whether it does, and makes you doubt the wisdom of the organization using the same tests as everyone else.'

In summary, when commenting on the overall fairness of the selection procedure, no one volunteered favourable comments about tests in either 1970 or 1974. Nine applicants in total ventured unfavourable comments about the use of tests (around 10 per cent of the total respondents): of these six had been offered jobs, three had been turned down. Further negative comments about tests were apparent when graduates offered advice on changing the procedure (although some advocated positive changes).

Many of the comments made about the 1970 procedure were taken into account when modifying it in subsequent years. The opportunity given to applicants of discussing the use of tests has tended to remove unrealistic doubts about it, while hopefully presenting an honest picture of the advantages and disadvantages of using tests in selection. This opinion is supported by the lack of specific comments about tests from 1974 respondents as compared with the 1970 respondents. However, an initial conclusion is that roughly 30 per cent of respondents choose to comment unfavourably about the use of tests in reply to free-response questions inviting criticism of the selection procedure.

MOTIVATIONAL DISTORTION

One of the drawbacks in the use of tests of 'typical' performance for selection is the possibility of an applicant distorting his responses to the items in order to present an 'ideal' profile. Three of the main ways of dealing with this are used here.

First, through the test patter and the form of administration it is hoped to remove as much mistrust as possible about the use of the test scores. Second, the test norms used are based on this applicant group (who might all be expected to distort their responses due to their perception of the situation as competitive). Third, a form of correction for faking is used based on the 'adjustment specification equation' approach outlined by Cattell *et al*. (1970, pp.149-50). Here, each individual's test profile is compared against the 'most ideal self' profile produced by Meredith (quoted in Cattell *et al*., p.54).

Using Cattell's method, a 'goodness of fit' index is produced which corresponds to the probability of the applicant having grossly distorted his responses to resemble the 'ideal'. In cases where this is thought to have happened, extra care is taken in drawing up a test report.

Three such cases occurred out of 96 applicants in 1974. In one case, the applicant's background indicated he was probably very close to being 'the ideal person'.

The specification equation used for estimating the probability of distortion was produced in the form:

$$Y = b_1 A + b_2 B + \ldots + b_{16} Q4 + a$$

where Y is an index of 'belongingness' to the group who might have distorted their 16PF responses to resemble their 'most ideal self'; this follows a Sten scale, with 10 or above indicating high belongingness and 0 indicating low belongingness to the 'most ideal self' group.

Using the procedure given by Cattell *et al.* (1970, pp. 149-50), the following equation was obtained:

$$\begin{aligned} Y = {} & 0.30A + 0.12B + 0.27C - 0.04E + 0.28F + 0.29G \\ & + 0.31H - 0.04I - 0.36L - 0.35M - 0.05N - 0.30O \\ & - 0.02Q1 + 0.28Q2 + 0.28Q3 + 0.30Q4 - 1.64 \end{aligned}$$

EVALUATION OF TESTS

Alongside the practical problems of administering a test procedure come the problems involved with validating it. Fortunately the procedure was drawn up with a particular validation model in mind. Mainly taken from Guion's work (1965), the approach is summed up neatly in Schein (1970, pp.22-3).

Four main steps are involved. First, develop criterion measures which sample effective job performance and select a research battery of tests which might predict this performance. Next administer the test battery to a group of applicants, but select without reference to their test scores. Third, collect criterion data, and correlate the predictors with the criteria. Finally, repeat the process on a different sample for cross-validation purposes.

Thus the model should have been easy to follow. The tests had been chosen to sample the types of job behaviour thought to be important for success in the company. Over a five-year period, 428 graduates were tested, with year-one test results locked away without being used (test data from the next four years seemed to play a minor role in the decision-making process). Supervisor ratings on 23 different scales were readily available on each graduate's staff-appraisal form (Ingleton 1973).

All that remained to be worked out were the separate correlations for each year. However, the reality of graduate selection seems to place severe constraints upon the usefulness of this approach. Indeed, the worth of this 'classical model' has been questioned by many recent publications in the area, e.g. Bray and Moses (1972), Campbell *et al.* 1970), Drenth (1971), McReynolds (1971).

The emphasis in selection research seems to be moving towards gaining a greater understanding of the many factors, both individual and organizational, which might affect the usefulness of any selection procedure. As Bray and Moses (1972) point out, 'There is (since 1968) a heightened awareness that selection procedures do not operate in a vacuum, but are part of a system.' In fact, these writers go so far as to abandon the use of the word criterion for the broader concept described as 'the distal end of the prediction equation'. In the case of graduate selection this seems to be the whole area, in both time and space, of subsequent job activity to which the successful graduate applicant will be exposed: the remainder of the selection procedure, training, the first job, the job environment and supervision, for example.

An emphasis on understanding what is going on rather than demonstrating significant correlations is also evident in Schmidt and Kaplan's (1974) approach. They comment that the degree of understanding attainable is a function of the predictor, as well as the criterion end of the prediction equation. In other words perhaps our test scores could be used to help us understand the way in which good performance in a job is assessed.

Experience in evaluating the procedure described here supports both the classical model and the newer approaches. For example, although 438 graduates were originally tested, obviously only a small proportion were offered employment. At the time of writing, only seven of these have personnel records which give an accurate picture of their current position and standard of performance.

Each of them is doing a different job, about which quite different kinds of objective performance data are available, and each job seems to require different kinds of behaviour. All are on very similar salaries, and on one of two staff grades (dependent more on their age and type of experience than on merit, probably).

Many more graduates are with the organization undergoing various forms of training. Thus, up to five years after selection the sample size makes it very difficult to correlate anything with anything to gain a meaningful result. However, at the other extreme, immediately after testing, we have a sample size of 428 whose test scores might be correlated with a criterion measure (whether a job offered or turned down by the selectors, for example). Here, of course, large-sample statistical techniques associated with the classical model can be applied.

Actual analyses carried out so far have been on the personality test data, and these can be considered under the two main headings of the 'understanding' approach (where large samples do not exist) and the 'classical' approach.

Immediate outcome validation ('a classical approach')
Immediately following the selection procedure, two types of criterion measure are available: was the applicant offered a job and, if offered, did he accept or decline the offer?

Was the applicant offered a job? For the five years 1970 to 1974, a complex (discriminant function) analysis was carried out to establish how well the test battery could distinguish, in advance, whether selectors would offer or not offer jobs to graduate applicants. Of course, the use of this criterion measure could be criticized for every year except 1970 (when test reports were withheld from selectors). This was because knowledge of test performance might well have influenced the interviewers' selection decision.

However, only in 1974 did the selectors seem to place any appreciable degree of reliance on the test report (see section on 'Reaction of line managers to tests').

In two years (1971 and 1973) the 16PF test was shown to discriminate between these two groups at better than chance level. However, as a cross-validation exercise this proved disappointing, since different values for the discriminant functions were apparent for each year.

If offered, did the applicant accept or decline the offer?
Here, similar discriminant analyses were carried out on the two groups, 'accepted offer' and 'declined offer' (see Figure 5:3). In four out of the five years, discrimination at significantly better than chance level has been possible.

Especially in 1973 and 1974, similar values for the discriminant functions have been established.

For instance, a discriminant analysis on the 1973 data yielded perfect discrimination between the two groups 'accept' and 'decline'.

In 1974, the 16PF scores of all applicants were fitted to the discriminant function equations produced in 1973, and a prior guess made for each applicant of whether he

Figure 5:3 Procedure for estimating the 'probability' of an applicant accepting or declining a job offer from his 16PF scores

The procedure used for estimating 'probability' of an applicant accepting or declining a job offer is taken from Dixon (1971, pp.196-203), using the BMD discriminant analysis program BMD05M.

First, the coefficients for the function discriminating the two groups 'accepted offer' and 'decline offer' were calculated, based on 1973 data. This gave the following equations: one for 'probability of accept'; one for 'probability of decline'.

'Probability of accept', based on 1973 data, is given by:

$P_i(A)$ = -180.26A +49.55B +356.49C -99.36E -221.03F
   +342.67G +476.27H -128.94I -222.27L +458.46M
   -64.96N +79.33O -27.89Q1 +240.07Q2 -150.39Q3
   +275.87Q4 -8782.62

'Probability of decline', based on 1973 data, is given by:

$P_i(D)$ = -167.46A +53.21B +333.62C -89.24E -202.78F
   +323.30G +443.42H -113.39I -205.32L +428.36M
   -56.84N +74.79O -19.69Q1 +226.38Q2 -145.75Q3
   +256.31Q4 -8020.75

where i = no cases, A = 16PF 'A' raw score, B = 16PF 'B' raw score, etc.

Following Dixon (p.202) two scores are computed for each applicant, and the larger is taken as indicating the group to which the applicant belongs (either 'accept' or 'decline'). Applying these equations to 1974 applicants, and relating predictions made to actual decisions, yielded the following contingency table for the 25 applicants offered jobs.

Predictions about decisions of those offered jobs in 1974

Actual	Predict decline job offer	Predict accept job offer	
Declined offer	8	3	11
Accepted offer	2	12	14
	10	15	25

The Fisher Exact Probability Test (Siegel 1956, pp.96-103) indicates that this finding is significant beyond the 0.01 level.

would accept a job if it were offered, or turn the offer down. The prediction was accurate in 80 per cent of the cases (as well as being statistically significant).

Thus it would have been possible, using the personality test data only, to achieve significant accuracy in predicting whether an individual who was offered a job in 1974 would accept that offer.

Since in most cases selection testing takes place in advance of the interview, such information might appreciably reduce interviewers' uncertainty over the final outcome of their selection decisions (i.e. over how many individuals would actually join the organization).

An attempt at explanation of this finding is difficult without further research. Two working hypotheses might explain it. First, that rather than measuring stable and persisting traits the 16PFQ is sampling a temporary 'state' of applicants of the kind, 'I'm not really sure I like this company.' This hypothesis is supported by the nature of the specification equation which does not rely on any single scale, but seemingly relates to every 16PF score - an overall pattern rather than a distinquishable 'type'.

Another view is that certain types of individual, as specified in a complex way by the 16PF profile, only accept jobs with large corporations. If this is the case, many ramifactions follow especially for vocational guidance for instance.

Further work is being carried out in an attempt to replicate this finding. No attempt has been made so far to communicate these predictions to selectors.

Longer-term validation (an 'understanding' approach)
This approach must, of necessity, rely on less precise information than immediate-outcome data, because of the small numbers of graduates involved, and the difficulty of measuring their performance.

So far, analysis has taken the form of comparing current staff-appraisal reports with narrative test reports prepared two or more years earlier but locked away immediately after the selection decision.

The degree of understanding obtained so far has, indeed, been more about the nature of the staff appraisal system than about the worth of the test.

In one case, where a graduate had a personality test profile indicating extreme shyness, the manager (two years later) seemed to be advocating taking up debating to cure this 'fault'. In another case, a narrative test report prepared before the selection interview read 'The low conscientiousness, high independence suggests that this individual will go his own way regardless of the rules.' Two years later, his manager seemed to criticize his general 'attitude' and suggested some form of 'discipline' was needed to straighten him out.

There is meant to be no criticism of the managers involved here, but certainly such findings might be fed back to managers on staff-appraisal courses run by the organization's training department.

Further analyses are planned here as and when more performance data are available but one thing is certain: it is not yet possible to use test scores to predict an individual's 'ultimate' level of achievement!

SUMMARY

Research into the use of tests is continuing in this organization - especially into the value of the 'optimum' performance tests which have not been the subject of much research as yet.

The major practical problem so far has involved the beliefs of line managers about the value of tests in selection, rather than in establishing predictive validities.

Great care must still be taken in the use of test results for selection decisions. This is partly because of the lack of evidence about their longer-term predictive validity, and partly because of the danger that too much emphasis might be placed on a test score, simply because it is seen to be 'objective'.

However, experience so far indicates that the selection tests do sample behaviour which occurs in the job situation (from a comparison of test reports and appraisal reports), and that these scores do act as signs that certain outcomes will occur following the testing situation, as the accuracy in predicting those who accept job offers signifies.

REFERENCES

Bray, D.W. & Moses, J.L.(1972), 'Personnel selection', *Annual Review of Psychology*, vol 23, pp.545-76

Cattell, R.B., Eber H.W. & Tatsuoka, M.M.(1970), *Handbook for the 16PF Questionnaire* (Champaign, Ill: IPAT)

Campbell, J.P., Dunnette, M.D., Lawler, E.E. & Weick, K.E. (1970), *Managerial Behaviour, Performance and Effectiveness* (New York: McGraw-Hill)

Cronbach, L.J. (1970), *Essentials of Psychological Testing*, 3rd edition (New York: Harper & Row)

Dixon, W.J. (1971), *BMD Computer Programs* (Berkeley, Calif: University of California Press)

Drenth, P. (1971), 'Theory and methods of selection', in *Psychology at Work*, ed. P.B. Warr (Harmondsworth: Penguin)

Guion, R.M. (1965), *Personnel Testing* (New York: McGraw-Hill)

Heim, A.W., Watts, K.P. & Simmonds, V. (1970), *Manual for the AH6 Group Test of High-Level Intelligence* (Windsor, Berks: NFER Publishing Co.Ltd)

Ingleton, C.C.P. (1972), 'A strategy for salesman selection', *Management Decision*, vol 10, pp.18-26

Ingleton, C.C.P. (1973), 'Performance appraisal data as criteria of work performance', paper presented to 6th Annual Conference of Occupational Psychology Section of the British Psychological Society, Lancaster University

McReynolds, Paul (ed.) (1971), *Advances in Psychological Assessment*, vol.2 (Palo Alto, Calif: Science & Behaviour Books)

Schein, E.H. (1970), *Organizational Psychology*, 2nd edition (Englewood Cliffs, NJ: Prentice-Hall)

Schmidt, F.L. & Kaplan, L.B. (1974), 'Composite vs. multiple criteria', in *Studies in Personnel and Industrial Psychology*, eds. E.A. Fleishman & A.R. Bass (Homewood, Ill: Dorsey Press)

Siegel S. (1956), *Nonparametric Statistics* (New York: McGraw-Hill)

Webster, E.C. (1964), *Decision Making in the Employment Interview* (Montreal: Industrial Relations Centre, McGill University)

6

The Use of Tests and Scored Questionnaires in Salesmen Selection
G. A. Randell

The selection of salesmen is a severe and continuing problem for most manufacturing organizations. Many studies have been undertaken to discover the attributes of successful salesmen and how they can be used in the selection situation. Over the years many assertions have been made about what it takes, in psychological terms, to be an effective salesman. Campbell and Campbell (1970), under the direction of the writer, published a bibliography of 235 references on salesmen selection. Of these, 95 references were specifically concerned with the attributes of successful salesmen.

In an early study reported by Moore and Hartman (1931) it was stated that, 'Intelligence and schooling seem to be of secondary importance for most selling positions, but an expansive, socialized, extraverted constitution is undoubtedly an asset.' Unfortunately little evidence was produced to support this assertion. This book also included discussion of the hereditary versus experience argument concerning salesmen. This is still a point of controversy. Sales managers can be heard stating that there are 'born' salesmen and that consequently sales training is a waste of time. The practical implication of this point of view is that all that needs to be done is to define the inborn characteristics, to identify their existence in an applicant in the selection situation and then to appoint to the task those people so endowed.

The basic assumption of this approach is that what it takes to be a salesman is one, or a group, of personality traits which are required for success in all selling jobs and that people either do or do not have them to a sufficient degree to cope with the work, or have them to a high degree and are consequently potential 'super-salesmen'.

An alternative view has been put forward by Guion (1965), who reviewed a wide range of studies concerning the characteristics which seem to go with effective sales performances. He summarizes his review with the remark that 'As a matter of fact, however, not only do sales jobs differ in terms of the commodity sold and its market, but they differ also in the psychological characteristics of the people who work in them.' The basic assumption of this approach is that what it takes to be a successful salesman is determined by the selling situation. This view implies that there is no such thing as an inborn or acquired trait of 'salesmanship'.

These two opposing views were put to the test in studies conducted over a period of five years by the Human Resources Research Group of the Management Centre of the University of Bradford. Findings from six groups of salesmen totalling 819 men will be discussed in this chapter. Four of the groups were within the gas industry, one was in the oil industry and one was from a tyre company. As much of their work was 'technical' selling there were similarities between the groups in terms of the sales methods used and the markets they worked in. One of the aims in choosing similar occupational groups was to discover if there was anything in the assertion that there are traits common to all salesmen. It was hypothesized that by picking such similar groups, if there were any psychological attributes common to all salesmen, it should at least show up in groups of relatively similar salesmen.

COLLECTING THE DATA

For each individual a comprehensive set of measures was collected. These measures can be categorized as:

1 Psychometric, i.e. measures of intelligence, aptitudes and other personality traits obtained, by means of standardized tests and scored questionnaires, by trained testers.

2 Biographical, i.e. information from an application form completed at the selection stage, or details held in personnel records.
3 Organizational factors, i.e. those aspects of the markets, and the management which could determine salesmens' performance, obtained from reports from the sales managers and marketing departments.
4 Criteria, i.e. measures that indicate how effectively a salesman is working, both in terms of the things that he has sold and the opinions of his manager or supervisor, obtained from commission and bonus records, sales reports, staff appraisal forms and specially designed supervisors' report forms.

Whenever possible a whole morning or afternoon testing session was arranged for up to twenty salesmen at a time. The session usually commenced with the researchers being introduced by a sales manager; then the researchers gave an explanation of the aims of the research. It was stressed to the salesmen that the test scores would be kept strictly confidential, and that only members of the research group would know them. They would be asked to put their names on each answer sheet as this would allow all the information collected about them to be brought together. Questions were then answered about the research project. It is gratifying to report that no salesman refused to cooperate in the research; on the contrary, a great deal of interest was expressed and encouragement given by the subjects to what they themselves realized to be an important and difficult project. The instruments were then administered by trained testers in accordance with the instructions laid down in the manuals.

TESTS AND QUESTIONNAIRES USED

To provide a broad base to the research a range of psychological tests and scored questionnaires were used. However, to provide some comparability all the salesmen completed the following:

1 Cattell Sixteen Personality Factor Questionnaire (16PF).
2 Allport-Vernon-Lindzey Study of Values.
3 Thurstone Interest Schedule.

In addition, according to the time available, the salesmen completed at least one of the following tests or questionnaires:

1. The Maudsley (or Eysenck) Personality Inventory.
2. Strong Vocational Interest Blank. This gives numerous measures of various occupational interests, but only the salesman scale was used.
3. Rosenzweig Picture-Frustration Study. Although this projective device is difficult to score it can provide nine measures of reactions to different kinds of mildly frustrating situations.
4. Raven's Progressive Matrices, 1938 edition.
5. Otis Quick-Scoring Mental Ability Test, Gamma A. This gives a single measure of 'mental ability'.
6. ACER Speed and Accuracy Test.

The biographical, organizational and criterion data were obtained by the research team from either existing record forms held within the organizations or by means of new forms. Such documents as application forms, staff appraisal forms, commission earnings, special bonuses and computer-produced sales figures were made available to the research team; in addition to these a specially designed subjective report form was completed by the sales manager for each man studied in the samples.

ANALYSING THE DATA

All these measures were submitted to various statistical analyses, using large electronic computers. It is not appropriate here to describe in detail the techniques used; they can be studied in my unpublished PhD thesis (Randell 1972).

The statistical findings for each group of salesmen studied and their practical significance were brought together in confidential reports to the sales management of the various groups of salesmen studied. The research team then met the senior management in each organization to discuss the personnel and organizational implications of the results.

FINDINGS AND OUTCOMES

The statistical output from the analyses was enormous. It would not be relevant for the purposes of this chapter to attempt to report them here. Consequently the main findings that were specifically useful for the senior management of each organization will be given, and the practical outcomes will be described.

A Gas (90 men)
The statistical findings indicated that the management of A Gas salesmen have reason to be confident that their assessment and control procedures are sufficiently sound for them to obtain useful indications of the performance of their salesmen at their job. As much of this performance information seems to be predictable from biographical and psychometric data the first main conclusion that was drawn is that it would be worthwhile to use the findings to develop the existing selection procedure for salesmen.

One of the main predictors of effective sales performance appeared to be the number of hobbies and interests a man has. When this was discussed with the sales management they realized that what they valued amongst their salesmen was the 'level of energy' that they applied to their work. There was a tradition of 'cold-calling' in the sales force; a salesman would be given the opportunity to enter an area and not only follow up leads gained from advertisements and enquiries at showrooms, but also take it upon himself to call on likely looking households in his attempts to sell gas appliances. This finding, therefore, indicated that the men who were energetic in their spare-time activities, with a wide range of hobbies, would also show similar effort and energy in their work. As the first way to develop the selection procedure would be to make the selection interview more purposeful, this finding could be used to form the basis of a more structured interview. Similarly, the indicators from the Thurstone Interest Schedule, in particular the relevance of 'business', 'executive' and 'physical science' interests and the additional implications of the Allport-Vernon 'Theoretical' scale, would give the interviewer more relevant topics to explore. There were also indications that some of the traits measured by 16PF could be of relevance. In particular, low scores on 16PF A(i.e. 'reserved/detached') appear to be related to average measures of salesmen's sales performance and their supervisors' subjective ratings; and low scores on the G factor (i.e. 'expedient') were related to measures of the salesmen's peak performance.

Therefore, the further conclusion was drawn that the 16PF could provide useful information to the selectors.

Consequently the management of this sales force decided to use the findings supplied from these analyses to develop their selection tools through a more structured interview and a scored questionnaire. They instituted a procedure to continue to collect follow-up information using both objective and subjective data derived from the specially designed follow-up report form as a source of validation data. This new procedure is now being subjected to a traditional validation study.

B Gas (99 men)
The findings of this group raised some interesting and important managerial problems. The statistical analyses showed that not much of work performance was predictable by the information collected from the salesmen by the tests and questionnaires. It was discovered that organizational and marketing factors were swamping the effects of the individual differences of the salesmen making up the sales force. When these findings were discussed with the management it emerged that current selling arrangements were organized on a team basis. Although the calls on potential customers were made individually, the day-to-day work was undertaken by a team of five or six salesmen, who met in the morning and planned to work together during the day, allocating calls and discussing approaches and results, in breaks between them. It therefore seemed probable that this group work was constraining any individual approaches that the salesmen may have had and which might have been more effective in particular selling situations. The suggestion was made that the significant negative correlations with previous sales experience were probably due to the fact that, within the groups, if any member started to boast about his methods of work in his previous employment he would probably have alienated his colleagues, who might then give him the less likely calls to make. This finding caused management to rethink their whole approach to team selling. In comparison with the A Gas group they did not seem to be making best use of the range of talents which may well have existed among their salesmen. They therefore decided to change to a more individually controlled sales procedure, so allowing the individual salesmen to plan their own daily sales arrangements, and to pay them commission as individuals, rather than in groups.

C Gas (266 men)
The test and questionnaire scores of this group indicated that the salesmen possessed characteristics that were significantly different from the 'general population'.

The scores also distinguished between different groups of salesmen within the sales force. However, the scores did not discriminate the better from the less-good sales performers. The reason for this appeared to rest with the quality of the criteria of sales performance used, rather than the relevance of the tests and questionnaires.

In comparison with the 'general population' these salesmen were more 'extravert', more 'intelligent', and had less 'clerical aptitude'. They placed more value on economic and political activities of life, but less on aesthetic, social and religious factors. They were more interested in work in the business category, and significantly less in humanitarian, artistic and musical activities.

Objective measures of sales performance (i.e. number and value of things sold) were not available for the majority of salesmen in this group. Where they were available only weak associations existed between them and subjective assessments i.e. ratings made about the men by their managers. There was one remarkable exception to this, and this concerned the group of salesmen who appeared to sell more gas cookers than anyone else in the sales force. This was a most perplexing finding and gave management considerable cause for thought. When the group was split in terms of good cooker salesmen and the rest, the good cooker salesmen turned out to be more conscientious, more controlled and socially precise, more satisfied with their job and older than average. This contrasted very markedly with the good salesmen of other appliances who appeared from the questionnaires to be more suspicious, more tense, more dissatisfied with their job and had been in the job longer than average. Looking at these findings it is not so remarkable after all that managers rated the cooker salesmen higher, since they appear easier to get on with and do the job without excessive complaint. Also it may be that there is something about selling cookers which makes it different from selling any other appliance. This could have been due to the higher commission rate and less public resistance to cookers which meant they were more attractive to sell. Further, cooker sales looked better on sales records because no purchase tax had to be deducted. Managers may therefore have tended to regard cooker salesmen more favourably and almost unconsciously gave them more encouragement. Consequently, those men who responded to this became progressively a more identifiable group. However, the above explanations were put forward as conjectures and as yet no completely satisfactory explanation has been found.

Within this sales force various other subgroups can be identified, according to the type of work and the place at which it was carried out. One of the subgroups mainly worked in showrooms. Members of this subgroup differed from the other sales representatives in various ways. An interest in biological sciences and humanitarian occupations seemed to be associated with the better showroom staff. Further, those staff who had low aesthetic values and a relaxed approach to problems were thought to be better salesmen by their sales supervisors.

When the different characteristics of the salesmen were correlated with aspects in their work environment some interesting and useful findings emerged. The organizational and job satisfaction questionnaires show differences in attitudes and expectations between the well-qualified relatively intelligent job groups within the sales force and the groups of salesmen who are less qualified and less intelligent. Higher intelligence seems to be associated with higher levels of job involvement and satisfaction and also with the need for participation in managerial decision-making. One of the most useful results obtained from the organizational questionnaires was an indication of a need to change the managerial methods and style of the sales management so that better use was made of the sales abilities existing in the sales force. Consequently it was recommended that the organization should develop training arrangements for the sales managers, on methods of man-management and control, which better matched the perceived needs of the various groups of salesmen. As the questionnaires had established a standard, any shifts in managerial style resulting from man-management training could be measured by re-administering the control style questionnaire. In this way the effects of the training could be directly assessed.

Another important training implication came from the confused picture which emerged from the analysis of the criterion measures. For the group with sales performance data there was little association between the men who sold well and the men managers perceived to be good at their job. It was therefore suggested that managers must revise their own criteria for evaluating effective sales staff. It was the inadequency of the criterion measures that probably accounted for the relatively low correlations that were obtained with the tests and questionnaires. Therefore, for this group the most practical implication of the findings was in the field of training activities for the sales managers and sales supervisors.

D Gas (175 men)
When the managers of this group were asked to list the importance of various characteristics of good salesmen they placed 'persistence in the pursuit of a sale' as by far the most highly regarded attribute of a good field salesman; whereas for showroom staff the most highly placed attribute was 'product knowledge'. As these judgments about what managers thought to be the most important behaviour associated with successful selling performance showed consistency through the regions it looked as if the managers could be making their judgments on some sound evidence. In this group the available measures of sales performance (i.e. value of things sold) were more objective than in C Gas and these objective criteria did correlate significantly with the subjective judgments of the managers. Consequently, in this sales force it looked as if more confidence could be placed in the ability of the managers to assess the performance of their salesmen on objective evidence rather than on personality traits.

The test and questionnaire scores indicated that the sales representatives judged as being more effective at their jobs were, in comparison with the rest of the group, less intelligent, more easily affected by feelings, more forthright, more dissatisfied with their work and more regular in their timekeeping. The showroom staff who achieved the best sales performances were significantly more self-confident, independent, materialistic, politically aware, and more satisfied with the content of their job. The better performers among district sales representatives were less readily definable and had less clear-cut results. However, the test and questionnaires indicated that the better district representatives had a high level of political awareness but were less economically oriented. In this group the more active the man was, as shown by the number of his hobbies, the higher he was regarded by managers. But the number of hobbies that a man had did not correlate with objective measures of his sales performance, so here again there may be some sort of halo effect associated with being an active man.

In this group, because of the many significant relationships between the questionnaire scores and the various kinds of sales performance measures, it was apparent that a selection procedure could be developed making use of the most significant scales of these questionnaires. It was therefore decided to recommend that local staff be trained to administer the relevant questionnaires in an attempt to develop the salesman selection procedure. Fortunately, the questionnaires which seemed to give the most useful insights into the characteristics of the more successful salesmen in this group, the Thurstone Interest Schedule and the Allport-Vernon Study of Values, are fairly easy to administer and use. Consideration was being given to incorporating these into the selection procedure and subsequently checking their effectiveness.

Tyremen (49 men)
The statistical findings from this group were surprising and so the management of the organization were asked to describe some of their most successful salesmen before the results were discussed with them. They were asked not to describe in general terms, but to have in mind particular individuals. The description that emerged of the successful salesman in this organization could be summarized by the phrase, 'a grey man'. This coincided with the overall description that could be drawn from the statistical analysis of the personality traits associated with successful sales performance within the sales force. From these findings the more successful salesmen appear 'humble', 'shy' and 'tenderminded', below average in intelligence for the group and with a tendency towards both intra- and extra-punitive responses to situations. This was so totally unlike the stereotype of the 'extraverted, happy-go-lucky, shrewd salesman' that it needed some careful explanation. The managers themselves suggested that, as they were by no means brand leaders in their market and their tyres were not widely advertised, the sales technique found to be most effective was for the salesman to 'hang around' tyre depots, hoping to solve some of the supply problems of the depot manager in meeting urgent orders. The company was able to provide a quick service in supplying tyres, being more flexible and centralized than its large competitors. Consequently the successful salesman of this group was not an energetic order-taker, but a quiet self-effacing man who was prepared to obtain his orders by merging into the background of the depot, rather than by any hard-selling techniques. Although this finding was shattering to the senior sales management of the company, who always envisaged their best salesmen to be of the typical bright, extraverted type (like themselves?) it did not come as a surprise to the area managers. This at least helped senior management to understand the kinds of people they were employing in

their sales force and who were most valuable to them. This finding also had implications to them for the design of their sales training courses.

Oilmen (140 men)
There were many significant and interesting inter-correlations among the variables studied in this group. Further, the existence of consistent relationships gave confidence that inferences drawn from the data were meaningful. For example, one small group of 19 salesmen had the responsibility for developing new outlets. They also had the highest mean 'anxiety' score of all the groups tested (as measured by the 'guilt prone' factor on the 16PF). This was explained by the fact that a decision had recently been announced to abolish their job, and obviously their anxiety about the future was being sampled by the researchers at the time of testing.

From the analyses two distinct groups of men could be identified, reflecting a division in the tasks the salesmen had to perform. The first group were the men who mainly dealt with shops. The successful representatives here were shown by the questionnaires to be more open, forthright and they tended also to be hard-headed, precise and reserved. This group also showed more significant interest in business matters. The other subgroup worked with larger outlets, such as garages. The more successful salesman here appeared to have the need to be a member of a team rather than a 'loner'; he would also tend to mix socially with colleagues and demonstrate other aspects of extraversion. This group was inclined to be more enthusiastic and had an interest in occupations requiring verbal ability.

Various regional differences emerged which seemed to provide some insights into the way in which the men in this group were treated by the organization. For instance, it became apparent that the salesmen from the regions differed in terms of their anxiety levels, perhaps providing an index of the amount of pressure they were under. Salesmen from the northeast of England and Scotland appeared to be under most pressure, while those from the Midlands and the northwest of England were under the least, as reflected by the 'anxiety' scores.

Another index here was the percentage of salesmen rated as 'potential managers' in each sales region. The northwest of England appeared to provide the highest proportion of potential managers (39 per cent of our sample were rated as management potential) whereas the southwest of

England had the lowest proportion (17 per cent). This probably reflected the tendency for individuals to prefer to remain in a salesman's job in the West Country and indicated probable pressure in a few years' time around the Lancashire area for managerial level appointments.

There were also regional differences in the scores from the test of reasoning ability. The mean scores of the regions on this test showed that the West Country had the highest scoring group of representatives, with Scotland and Northern Ireland having the lowest mean scores.

These findings gave the regional sales managers opportunities for much debate, and removed some mythology from the organization, although the absence of any agreed explanations of these findings did not enable any managerial decisions to be made.

The important practical implication of the study of these salesmen was the development of a more structured selection interview, based on an agreed interview record form, which would help the regional managers to go about selecting their salesmen in a more systematic and purposeful way. This was done by first producing a special report and manual on the findings and their practical implications which was issued to all sales managers. Care was taken to make this report readable and attractive. It gave detailed guidelines on how to assemble information from applicants under the headings of the key characteristics of the more successful salesman, as identified by the research. A programme of training for regional sales managers in selection interviewing was then instituted. It was based on a videotape made by the research group on the skills of collecting data from people by means of the interview, and involved extensive practice of the skills involved.

An additional outcome for this organization was the information this research gave about the working of the staff appraisal scheme. The findings showed that many decisions about the development of the staff were being based on possibly irrelevant personality traits. This supported internal pressures from the staff of the company to make considerable changes in their staff appraisal and development scheme. The findings of the research therefore provided the final impetus for a change in the management development procedure in this company.

GENERAL CONCLUSIONS

In the above results no general trait of salesmanship has

emerged. What it takes to be a 'good' salesman is different in each organization studied. This finding has supported Guion's (1965) viewpoint quoted earlier.

However, the results have shown that by studying the salesmen making up each sales force by means of tests and scored questionnaires a great deal of knowledge can be gained about the nature of the sales force and their selling problems. This knowledge can be used to suggest arrangements that will make better use of the abilities and interests of the salesmen already employed. This leads to the important conclusion that when attempting to develop a strategy for salesman selection it would be better to concentrate on matching particular types of people to particular types of selling occupations within existing sales organizations, rather than attempting to set up any general salesman selection procedure (see also Ingleton 1972). The search for the use of any general traits of 'salesmanship' would seem to be less useful to selling organizations than attempts at matching people to specific sales jobs. From this the general implication emerges that organizations should be cautious about appointing salesmen just on the grounds of their previous sales experience.

The kinds of analyses described in the above research make it possible to develop a selection procedure appropriate to the needs of the organization. Such a procedure would certainly make use of the findings generated by the kinds of tests and questionnaires used in the studies described here. In a summary report to the gas industry a structure for a general selection procedure for salesmen was recommended. The report indicated how test and questionnaire data could be used in conjunction with interview and other information.

The studies described in this chapter indicate that standardized tests and scorable questionnaires can play a crucial part in revealing the basic information concerning the individuals making up an organization. It is from this information that plans can be made for developing both the selection procedure for acquiring sales staff and the organization's methods for making the best use of its sales force. It is stressed that getting the work organization right is the first objective, and that once this has been achieved then people can be selected, trained and developed in the light of an effective organizational structure. This is arguably the most realistic approach to individual and organization development. The projects described in this chapter were aimed at achieving these objectives. What has been demonstrated is that effective personnel selection is just one aspect of organization development. It is unwise for personnel selection specialists to think that just to get the right people for a job is sufficient to ensure effective work performance. The use of a battery of tests and questionnaires cannot only indicate the kinds of people that would be most suited for a particular job, but can also demonstrate if the organization is making best use of the people that it already employs.

REFERENCES

Campbell, I. & Campbell, J. (1970), *A Selected Bibliography of Material Related to Salesmen Selection* (Bradford: University of Bradford Human Resources Research Group)

Guion, R.M. (1965), *Personnel Testing* (New York: McGraw-Hill)

Ingleton, C.C.P. (1972), 'A strategy for salesman selection', *Management Decision*, vol.10, pp.18-26

Moore, B.V. & Hartman, G.W. (eds.) (1931), *Readings in Industrial Psychology* (New York: Appleton)

Randell, G.A. (1972), 'An application of scientific and technological concepts to a problem of worker behaviour', unpublished PhD Thesis, University of London Library

7

Selecting Engineers in an Electronics Firm

J. Copeland

Our company is a long-established specialist electronic business in the high-employment home counties. In the early 1960s the training department had selection problems basically different from those of the engineering industry in general. We were, and are, operating in a fast-growing and rapidly changing technology, namely electronics. We needed young men who could proceed after training to one of three broad task areas which the manufacture of electronic equipment then involved. These areas were:

1 Instrument making.
2 Prototype wiring.
3 Testing, fault-finding and calibration.

Of these three areas, the first used fairly conventional and static techniques. The second was beginning to change from point-to-point wiring between component-board assemblies as the use of printed-circuit boards increased rapidly (although thin-film techniques were a somewhat hazy dream). An essential skill was the ability to translate both ways between circuit diagrams and hardware. Test technicians then, as now, worked in the third area of assessing equipment performance relative to specification, and identifying and rectifying faults. In addition to understanding circuit diagrams in terms of hardware, these people needed a good grasp of circuit principles and the techniques of electronic measurement, as well as an appreciation of the somewhat abstract concepts of basic electronics. Both test staff and prototype wiremen also needed the capacity to progress from circuits using valves and discrete components, via printed circuit boards abounding in transistors, to integrated circuits with the associated 'systems' style of thinking.

Important restraints existed in the size of our yearly intake and our training facilities. An intake of fifteen to sixteen a year total for all three categories was usual and, of these, usually only seven or eight became good test technicians.

Our selection methods then included an intelligence test (AH4), an essay, a progressive mathematics paper covering from simple vulgar fractions to simultaneous equations, and an interview. This procedure was weighted in favour of the interview, but rarely enabled us to pick out those youngsters who could survive both the on-the-job training and the academic courses run by the local college of further education. Too often we selected people with apparent academic and/or practical promise which failed to materialize.

In 1963, the National Foundation for Educational Research (NFER) approached the local college to ask whether they and the local employers would take part in a pilot scheme of research into the problems and relative merits of day release and block release. The results were later published by Moore (1969). During this research each boy would be tested, and his progress in subsequent years followed by sample interviewing and noting his record of academic and work progress.

We agreed to take part. In due course each boy attending the college was asked to sit the Morrisby Differential Test Battery (Morrisby 1955), the results of which were confidential to the researchers. Members of the staff of the NFER also interviewed a number of the boys.* Some time later, these members of NFER enquired of us about lads who had failed exams, or left the company, or had passed to other colleges. It became increasingly obvious that these interviewers (who seemed to be exclusively young Australian lasses with no knowledge or experience of electronics) knew more than we did about many aspects

*The same college had also cooperated with NFER in a large-scale study (as yet unpublished) of apprentice selection which began in 1958. Some of the interviews referred to were in conjunction with that study. (Editor)

of the behaviour of our apprentices and trainees. Even with those they had never interviewed or met themselves, they were aware of behaviour characteristics which we were just discovering after a couple of years or so. Asked how they reached their conclusions, their reply was inevitably, 'His DTB would suggest...', or 'Looking at his DTB profile it seems that...', and so on. Intrigued and curious, we began to think that this DTB might help in answering the two major questions of selection:

1 Has the applicant the necessary capability?
2 If so, how will he use it?

Since, however, we had a practical - but sceptical - outlook, and a mistrust of large-scale statistics about individuals, the only way to evaluate this DTB (or indeed any other test) was to use it and see what happened.

After suitable training we applied the DTB in 1964 to all craft and technician applicants. However, the results were not used, selection continuing on the old system. Quite separately the DTB profiles were interpreted. They suggested rejection of two or three of the candidates and before the end of their first year we realized the correctness of these recommendations. Had we taken notice of the test results in selection we could have avoided situations that were difficult for both the company and the boys.

We could now, with confidence, exclude those who - after a very promising start - become first an annoyance to supervisors and finally to themselves and their fellows. To assist the education and training department in its understanding and interpretation of profiles, a number of company personnel from all levels also sat the test battery on a personal and confidential basis. In all succeeding years our basic method of craft and technician trainee selection has been the DTB followed by an interview.

THE MORRISBY DIFFERENTIAL TEST BATTERY

The Morrisby Differential Test Battery contains twelve tests, each of which measures a different aspect of an individual's mental make-up. The results are presented as a histogram or profile; Figure 7:1 is a typical profile.

The test author has carefully matched the separate tests statistically; probably it is the only such matched battery in existence. The differential relationships, both between the twelve test scores and within and between various groupings of them, provide most of the significant information about the test subject. Profile

Figure 7:1 A typical DTB profile

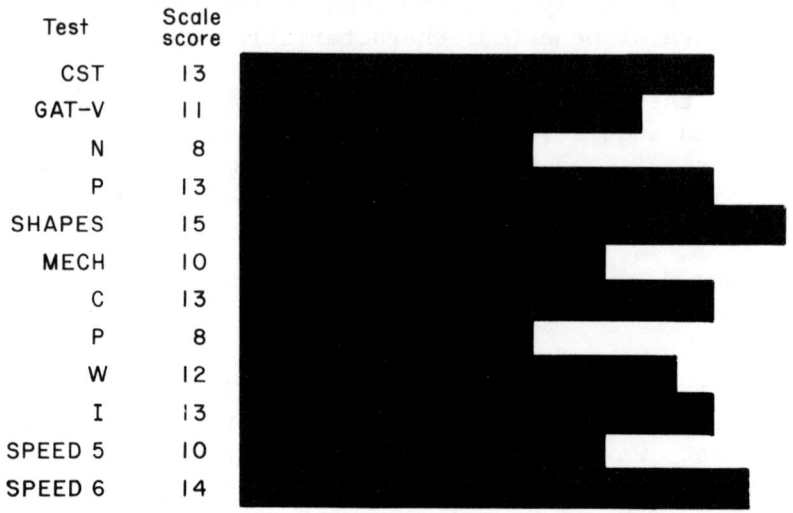

Test	Scale score
CST	13
GAT-V	11
N	8
P	13
SHAPES	15
MECH	10
C	13
P	8
W	12
I	13
SPEED 5	10
SPEED 6	14

interpretation is a developing technique and J.R. Morrisby is continually collecting results and other relevant information. We are still extending our own knowledge and experience.

A clear note of warning is necessary; these profiles do *NOT* give a clear-cut, black and white, sharp image of a person's mental characteristics and behaviour, but they do very reliably indicate tendencies, preferences and recurring thought habits.

The test instruments are not of the kind usually associated with the field of 'personality' testing.

The first of the tests, the Compound Series Test (CST) is also the longest, the time allowed being thirty minutes. It provides a buffer and introduction to the rest of the battery.

The next three tests - Verbal, Numerical and Perceptual General Ability Tests (GAT-V, GAT-N, GAT-P) - have content similar to that found in more conventional intelligence tests. Each has three parts, each testing different aspects of the respective mental function.

The next two, SHAPES and MECHanical, assess spatial perception and comprehension of mechanical principles.

The second half of the profile is provided by the six speed tests. Of these, the first four provide the 'Modal Profile', that is the habitual mental behaviour of the test subject. The final two tests are a measure of manual dexterity; the first of dexterity with minimal conscious control, the second of dexterity with great intellectual control.

For simplicity the profile may be considered as in two parts. The first six tests give an indication of mental ability; the remaining six speed tests provide information about significant characteristics of behaviour.

The ability block

The three General Ability Tests give four basic profiles shown in Figure 7:2.

Figure 7:2 Four basic profiles from the ability block of the DTB

GAT-V ▬ N ▬▬ P ▬▬▬	Science	People who tend to prefer to get their theory through practical experience. They have a 'finding-out by doing' approach which prefers science subjects and direct methods of learning, rather than theoretical bookish methods.
GAT-V ▬▬▬▬ N ▬▬ P ▬	Arts	People who tend to prefer the conventional teaching method, with the emphasis on being taught rather than on learning, and arts subjects
GAT-V ▬▬ N ▬▬▬ P ▬▬	Commerce	People who tend to quantify or grade information and things whenever possible; who are more concerned with the organization of method or system, rather than with its end product; who quickly grasp the significance of numbers
GAT-V ▬▬▬ N ▬▬ P ▬▬▬	Social Service	People who are at home with either 'theoretical' or 'experience-based' approach. Usually concerned about people, either in mass or as individuals. They often prefer such school subjects as biology or geography.

Other GAT profile combinations occur, and patterns have been established, for example, for computer programmers, journalists and biological scientists.

The GAT results may be compared differentially with the CST. When the latter predominates it usually means that the person has not habitually used, and probably is not using, all available mental potential. Generally he has not learned how, as a matter of habit, to harness his full mental power. Such a person's performance of real, 'on-the-job' tasks tends to exceed that in the unreal 'academic' or training task.

In the reverse case, when the CST is lower, performance on the job may disappoint those who know his academic or training-course performance. Since he is likely to work habitually at full mental capacity, he has little if any potential for further development.

SHAPES/MECH form a subunit indicating, among other things, practical ability and the usual approach to problems. When the SHAPES score is the larger, the person tends to adopt an 'overall-look' method which keeps the whole problem in view. With MECH higher, there is a tendency to see the trees rather than the wood and to break problems down into definable parts which can be dealt with in a routine manner.

These first six mental ability tests, considered as a block, give not only the person's preferred or most appropriate field of activity, but also indications of his general approach to tasks, as shown in Figure 7:3.

The modal profile

This is provided by the first four speed tests which are called: Concept Speed, Perseveration, Word Fluency, Ideational Fluency.

Concept Speed indicates speed of understanding and decision. Perseveration provides a measure of mental inertia - how slowly or quickly thoughts can be switched or mental habits changed. Word Fluency (from a simple word-making test experienced in an open-ended ambiguous situation) reflects the degree of emotional certainty or inner confidence. Ideational Fluency (how fast simple ideas can be produced in an open-ended ambiguous situation) reveals mental fluidity or drive and reflects demonstrated confidence.

Any of these four taken alone means very little, but, looked at as a block, their differential scores give eleven basic modes of (probable) mental behaviour shown in Figure 7:4.

Figure 7:3   Indications of general approach to tasks

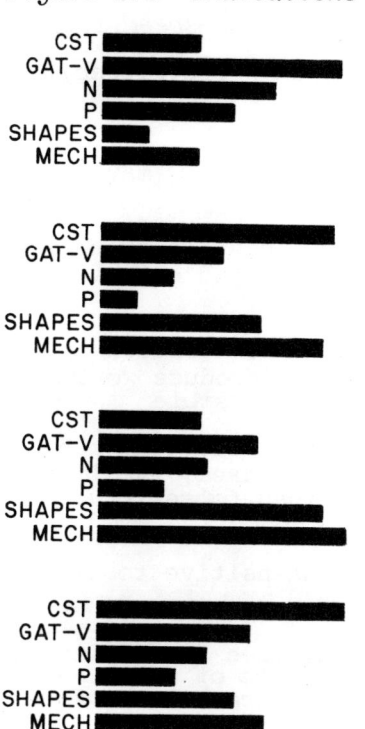

Academic, theoretically minded about problems

Non-scholastic, practically minded about problems

Orientation towards tasks; 'green-fingered', thinks with his hands

Instant understanding, performance poor without the challenge of a 'real' task

Dexterity
The remaining two speed tests, 5 and 6, show the level of dexterity and whether it is of a 'speed' or 'skill' type (see Figure 7:5).

It is often not realized in our society, so strongly oriented to written examinations, that handwriting capability can account for as much as 20 per cent of a person's examination performance.

The whole profile
Comparison of the whole ability block with the modal block shows whether 'mind' or 'personality' tends to dominate the behaviour. When the ability block is dominant, solving problems or getting at the 'truth' of situations can provide a sufficient reward in itself. When

Figure 7:4 Modal profiles: basic modes of probable mental behaviour predicted by the first four speed tests

C = Concept Speed; P = Perseveration; W = Word Fluency;
I = Ideational Fluency

1. Reasonable and decisive approach to situations, flexible mind; may appear detached

2. Similar to 1, but less flexible; prefers to follow rules and established practice

3. So flexible that concentration on one task long enough to produce worthwhile results is impossible

4. Conformist; an 'organization' man; operates well in relaxed, familiar situations; inclined to seize up under stress

5. Overconfident; insensitive to situations; talkative

6. Lacks confidence; does not really believe himself capable of doing anything; may become agressive - often verbally - if pushed

7. Rigid; an extreme version of 2; once having accepted an idea or system finds it virtually impossible to change to another

8. Grasps ideas easily and likes modifying them to personal notions but, having little persistence, is too easily satisfied by first efforts

9. Slow on the uptake with a preference for the tried and trusted routine. In extreme cases, will not try anything new. Will always attempt perfection, practising in private before allowing others to know

10. Usually shows a rather negative or uncooperative attitude. Having acquired a 'book of rules' adheres to it through thick and thin

11. Great tenacity and singleness of purpose, particularly when this block dominates the whole profile

Figure 7:5 Profiles from the dexterity speed tests

SPEED 5 ▇▇▇▇▇▇▇▇▇
SPEED 6 ▇▇▇▇▇

'Speed' Ladies with this profile would have a preference for knitting, as against embroidery; handwriting not very legible; somewhat impatient

SPEED 5 ▇▇▇▇▇
SPEED 6 ▇▇▇▇▇▇▇▇▇

'Skill' Embroidery preferred to knitting; legible, if not always beautiful, writing; patient

the modal block is higher, visible personal success and status appear to be more important. This relationship between the blocks also shows the relative importance of the modal characteristics in determining behaviour.

Summary
The above description gives only a very brief account of the information obtainable from the Differential Test Battery. A more extended discussion of the test can be found in Goode (1969). Unlike many other tests, it is person-oriented rather than task-oriented. It gives a reliable indication of a person's effective capability but, of course, does not indicate his circumstances - family or work environment, times of particular stress, motivation, etc - which should be assessed by interview or other means. Very often it does suggest that certain situations, or perhaps motivation, may be of special significance for a particular person.

OTHER TESTS

Additional tests can prove helpful by providing further information. Among those we have used are the Rothwell-Miller Interest Blank and the Morrisby Career Interest Test.

For very special cases, when personal counselling is sought, we use the Morrisby Personal Questionnaire, designed to supplement the DTB in counselling situations. This is a booklet which is completed in a person's own time; it also contains the Career Interest Test. The first part uses simple but carefully graded and constructed questions that enable the person completing it to think very clearly through his own activities, satisfactions and achievements.

A completed Personal Questionnaire enables the counsellor to get to basic facts and problems more quickly and more effectively than by the usual progressive interview.

USING THE TESTS

Selection

All craft, technician and student trainees and apprentices are selected using our standard method of a DTB followed by interview. The information from the profile is available at the time of interviewing, and this enables the interviewer to suit his approach and questions to the applicant. A striking example of how useful this can be was provided by a student apprentice applicant whose DTB profile is shown in Figure 7:6.

Figure 7:6 Profile of an applicant for a student apprenticeship

An interviewer at another company where the battery is not used had written of him 'Hasn't really much idea - a drifter. Doesn't really know why he wants to do engineering; doesn't really know why he is applying for university; doesn't know why he likes 'progressive pop'; no initiative, not even very bright.'

This account did not seem to us to tally very well with some of the information on his application form. The profile suggests why: the very low Word Fluency test score indicates an absence of emotional certainty or inner confidence. Such a person will not be happy in the one-to-one interview which quickly probes the limits of his knowledge.

Very aware of his own shortcomings and lack of certain items of knowledge, he will condemn himself and withdraw mentally from the interview. Forearmed with such knowledge, it was possible to lead him gently, via his delight in electronics as a hobby, to discuss such things as his inability to spell and the problems this has caused him from time to time. An enthusiastic amateur electronics engineer with a suitably practical outlook, he had a great interest in the field of control engineering. Several of his achievements in that line were remarkable for a schoolboy. Yet the first interviewer, an experienced and sympathetic interviewer by normal standards, had discovered none of it.

For people with modal profiles 10 or 11 (Figure 7:4), motivation is very important. The interview can be oriented towards discovering whether they know what they want to do and, if so, whether their aims are compatible with what you want them to do in the proposed job. If these aims do not coincide, the interviewer must estimate the chances of either converting the person to wanting that job, or of changing the job to suit the person's aims; no other possibility is likely to work for long.

The information from the profile is obviously useful in the case of those with speech defects, when interviewing can be extremely difficult and embarrassing, if not impossible.

Also, of course, for most of the modal profiles given, having such information before an interview allows one more time to investigate knowledge, skills and the various aspects of motivation more effectively and objectively.

Training

The knowledge of trainees gained from their DTB profiles reduces almost to zero the time taken by instructors to get to know each individual's attitudes and approach. The perfectionist (modal profile 9) will not, perhaps, attempt an exercise if he does not feel he can do it. The scatterbrain (modal profile 3) tries to rush in all directions at once. The solitary worker (modal 6) will rarely ask questions in a group, finds it impossible to learn from the experience of others and needs to do everything himself. The success- or status-conscious person (modal 10) must feel both that he is achieving and that his progress is recognized by others if he is to continue to make an effort.

Such knowledge about individuals - and it is objective

knowledge, not subjective opinion - is invaluable to instructors and is equally useful to the trainees themselves, if they can understand and accept it; the profile, of course, indicates the likelihood of such acceptance.

Much of our experience of interpreting profiles was gained in our training centres, by relating trainees' behaviour and performance of tasks to their profiles. Indeed, it was here that we first fully realized the continuing significance of the profiles as a diagnostic tool; they were relevant not only for selection but also for understanding the learning problems of trainees. They enabled us to predict a person's likely reaction to, and difficulties in, certain group working situations; we could help trainees to evaluate their problems and appreciate their strengths. We began to use the mass of selection information in a positive way to increase the achievement of trainees, thus making company training more effective.

This has continued, and the DTB helps instructors to a better understanding both of themselves and of their trainees, so that learning becomes a person-oriented activity in which each trainee takes an active rather than a passive part. We aim to create situations in which the individual's particular problems can be accepted and understood rather than be brushed aside, hidden or ignored.

One example is that of a young man who could, and did, demonstrate his considerable knowledge either on a bench or in oral answer to technical questions, but who failed quite simple examination papers. Discussion, triggered by the modal profile 9 (a perfectionist attitude), shown in Figure 7:7, revealed that he was ashamed of his inability to spell. As a result, when writing answers to examination questions, he tried to use only those words he was confident he could spell; a time-wasting procedure leading to continued failure.

Figure 7:7 Profile of a perfectionist

We were able to convince him that correct spelling was of far less importance than the communication of his knowledge. His acceptance that difficulty with spelling is quite common - some members of the training staff having such problems - produced a great improvement almost at once. He used a much larger vocabulary which was spelt correctly! We might have discovered his problem without his DTB result, but not so quickly or effectively. Perhaps more importantly, we should not so easily have known the extent of his under-achievement in written work and we could not have demonstrated it so clearly to him.

Supervision
In areas of the company outside our training centres, we have been able to help some managers and supervisors to a better understanding of their subordinates. All too often the working supervisor loses objectivity when dealing with his workforce under the pressures and stresses of meeting cost and output targets; often the working relationship with a new employee is ruined in the first few weeks. For example, a new recruit will occasionally be the type of person who needs time to adjust to new situations; given this time, such a person can become a loyal and diligent worker. Providing his supervisor has been warned of this tendency and allows for it, all will be well; if, however, it is unknown or ignored, the new employee could degenerate into a stubborn and unsatisfactory misfit. Using DTB results renables one to provide such warnings.

Counselling
From time to time it becomes necessary to help a trainee or member of one's staff to cope with a personal problem - in or out of work - which is reducing his work efficiency. Knowing the DTB profiles of those for whom one is responsible enables one to counsel much more effectively in such situations. For example, a person with modal profile 6 faced with a difficult problem is likely to try to rationalize it away and can even be dishonest to himself in order to avoid facing up to the reality of failure. During this process such a person may adopt an agressive attitude which - if one is not prepared for it - can prevent effective counselling.

CONTRIBUTION FROM THE DTB

The Differential Test Battery was initially used for the selection of craft and technician apprentices, indeed for all male applicants in the 15-16 age range who were applying for any training vacancies.

Next we used it for the adult technician trainees and learned to use it positively as an aid to the training process. In 1968 we began testing student apprentice applicants and, in 1970, graduates at their in-company interviews following the milk round. In both these last two groups a selection is made before testing; this pre-selection is based on the candidate's expressed preferences, hobbies, interests and academic record as given on an application form and on other written information - such as a headmaster's report in the case of students.

Various members of the managerial staff have been tested, as have many of the sales engineers. Some of these people took the test in order to understand the test results better, thereby gaining a better appreciation of the abilities and aptitudes of their own staff. Other managers have requested the help of the training staff when wishing to promote or discuss the career path of a subordinate. Most recent recruits to the sales staff have attended for test after a preliminary interview.

Any evaluation of the contribution made by the DTB to the efficiency of our selection and training methods must be largely subjective. This is so for two main reasons:

1. We are a manufacturing company not a psychological research organization, and the collection of recruitment, attainment, effectiveness and other relevant statistics is an interesting but very time-consuming exercise.
2. For the purposes of statistical validity, we are not able to follow up that majority of applicants whom we turn down. Also, the vagaries of the industrial climate, the advent of population bulges, and such national policies as ROSLA, inevitably cause variations which are very complex. These would need careful unravelling in order to achieve any worthwhile statistical analysis.

Recruitment and selection
The most significant contribution in this area has been to company reputation; in spite of zero advertising expenditure, the number of craft and technician apprentice applicants has shown a steady increase over the years. This increase has been maintained although other companies operating in the same field of engineering have had great difficulty in attracting suitable applicants.

In the case of the adult technician training exercise already described, it is difficult to see how the selection would even have been possible without the use of the battery. Of the 40 originally selected, 32 completed the course and 12 were still with us after six years despite the very great national demand for persons with even rudimentary electronic knowledge and skills. Several of these first adult trainees now hold positions of technical supervisory responsibility.

Among our technician apprentices a relatively high proportion are academically successful, in terms of obtaining Final Telecommunications Technicians' Certificates. Those completing the course, but who are less capable academically, are much in demand by the supervisors of our electronic test departments. We have virtually eliminated candidates who shine at interview but later cannot produce a sustained effective performance.

The one-year Ordinary National Certificate course was based on the selection by DTB from among student applicants of those whose practical engineering ability meant that they were unsuitable for the highly academic attitudes prevailing in many sixth forms. This scheme allows us an additional year in which to help the good practical engineer, capable of complex electronic design and development work, sort out his educational problems after failing his 'A' levels. It is significant how often such good, practical engineers produce poor academic results, yet receive comments of 'excellent' about their project work. The company has sponsored a number of such young men to sandwich degree courses; some, who have refused the offer of a degree course, have remained with us to become excellent technician engineers.

Academic qualifications

Using the DTB allows us to keep formal academic qualification, by C.S.E., O and A Levels, or degree, in true perspective. The profiles show how high academic achievement does not necessarily foretell good on- job performance in industry.

In the case of engineering graduates, the average of the first four tests of the DTB spread over a surprisingly wide range - scale scores 6 to 20, with the majority clustered around 15. The large number between 10 and 12, technician ability to us, suggests poor university selection; a suggestion supported by the 25% to 30% first year failure rate at such places.

Interviewing technique

A very significant gain from the use of the DTB has been an enormous improvement in the art of interviewing. From studying the test result profile, one can modify the interview to suit the particular applicant. Also, being released from the need to explore potential ability and some of the significant aspects of personality, one can give more time to exploring motivation. A few examples may help by demonstrating the usefulness:

1. A person with a modal profile of type 4 will almost always first tell the interviewer of his failures, and may have to be gently persuaded to discuss his successes.
2. A type 5 profile will be cheerful and optimistic and chatter happily about anything; indeed, it may prove difficult to confine him to a specific subject in order to explore depth of knowledge.
3. A type 2 is likely to be slow in answering questions and concerned that the answer given is as accurate as possible. Abrupt changes of topic are likely to slow him down.

Preknowledge of this kind of information allows the interviewer to create a situation in which the candidate can quickly gain confidence and can discuss his motivations and ambitions much more frankly and clearly than is usual in the normal interview.

Training methods

I discussed earlier the adult technician training course which was when we first realized the significance for our training methods of the DTB information. From this original, and now to us rather crude, beginning we have developed a system of programmed instructional modules which enable students over a wide range of ability levels to develop electronic knowledge and practical skill, particularly in the field of measurement. Each programme is arranged to allow the student to proceed from practice to theory, or vice versa, according to preference. Either way he gains an appreciation and understanding of the real relationship between these two.

FUTURE PLANS

We plan to continue to use DTB and other selection information to improve our training methods and work relationships. The root of much industrial unrest seems to us to lie in the inadequate practical understanding of human relationships. One of our ambitions is to find enough time to run a group training course for supervisors, along structured T-group lines, but based on course members' DTB profiles. We believe that such a situation would emphasize the importance of self-knowledge and self-acceptance, as well as of the acceptance of others as they are and not as we might like them to be. The practical appreciation and understanding of people gained by letting course members discuss for themselves the significance of a variety of group tasks could only lead to better communication, more objective judgments and decisions, and more efficient use of the abilities of others.

CONCLUSION

We have collected few statistics for analysis. As already mentioned, we are aware that such data as we could assemble would not be complete since a majority of those tested do not join the company. Also we would like to emphasize that the battery, providing as it does twelve separate test results, with the various patterns of their cross-differential relationships also providing a wealth of information, is a comprehensive measure of people, their abilities, aptitudes and tendencies. From an early scepticism we have come to accept that the DTB provides a reliable and accurate way of looking at people. It is not a task-oriented test system where 'The Test' is a kind of fixed-size filter through which applicants must pass. Rather, it provides the means for enabling people to maximize their contribution in fields suited to their particular talents. The real proof of a pudding is in the eating; the real proof of tests is the contribution their use provides.

REFERENCES

Goode, Bill (1969), 'Aptitude-oriented training techniques', *Industrial Training International*, May, pp.206-9.

Moore, B.M. (1969), *Day or Block Release* (London: National Foundation for Education Research)

Morrisby, J.R.(1955) *The Differential Test Battery* (Hemel Hempstead: Educational and Industrial Test Services)

Morrisby, J.R.(1969) *The Theory of the Differential Test Battery* (Hemel Hempstead: Educational and Industrial Test Services)

8

Choosing Tests for Clerical Selection

Kenneth M. Miller

PURPOSES OF THE STUDY

The two examples of the introduction of testing in the clerical field to be described in this section, arose for quite different reasons. In the first case, the Sun Alliance and London Insurance Group, which had recently moved its main clerical operations 40 miles from London, wished to appoint more married women to its staff. However, most of the women who were applying to the group either had left school prior to the introduction of the GCE or had not stayed long enough at school to take formal examinations.

For present school leavers the possession of acceptable educational qualifications is still the main criterion for obtaining an interview.

The request was for a short battery of clerical tests which could be administered when a married woman (and probably in due course other applicants without the required educational subjects) applied for a job. The tests and interview would need to be completed in an hour or less.

The second company was a large mail order firm with a number of locations in the northwest of England whose stimulus to seek the introduction of tests was high labour turnover. Their request was also for a short battery.

In both companies, tests are seen as supplementing the information obtained in interview and on the application form. The insurance company wanted to extend its labour pool while the mail order company wanted to reduce labour turnover and also to obtain a better quality of staff to be ready when an impending change to a computerized system occurred.

The insurance company, as well as wanting tests for selection of clerical staff, also has a consultant psychologist to oversee the administration of, and be responsible for, the interpretation of tests of ability and personal characteristics completed by applicants for graduate traineeship. He has also assisted with the introduction of tests for professional trainees.

The mail order company intends to extend the use of tests to other categories of staff. The second category to be considered will probably be visual display unit operators who are responsible for transferring data to a computer.

Part of the purpose of the presentation of these two case studies is to show how a larger group of tests was reduced to an effective short test battery.

In each organization the analysis of the work (carried out a year apart) led to putting together two overlapping groups of tests. The suggested group of tests (shown in Figure 8:1) was determined after studying the work, discussing demands of the job with personnel officers, managers and immediate supervisors, observing people at work and talking with them.

SAMPLES

In the insurance company a minimum sample of 70 was requested. This contained 22 males and 48 females. The sample was drawn by the investigator on a random basis from nominal lists provided by the office supervisor.

The mail order company operated in 6 locations but it was only possible to draw the sample from 4 of these. The staff of the company considered that these locations covered the full spectrum of the labour force. The aim had been to draw 40 staff from each location, half aged 24 or younger and half aged 25 and older: half rated as good or very good and half with lower ratings. The final sample consisted of 148 with 34,37,38 and 39 respectively from each location. 80 were aged 24 or younger and 68 were older. 77 were rated in the top two groups and 71

Figure 8:1 Groups of tests suggested for two users

Attribute Tested	Insurance Test used	Mail order
Verbal ability	Test of Mental Alertness - Verbal and PTI - Verbal	PTI - Verbal
Numerical ability	Test of Mental Alertness - Quantitative	-
Intelligence/mental alertness	Test of Mental Alertness - Total	-
Clerical accuracy (Number and name checking)	ACER Speed and Accuracy	EITS Clerical 1
Immediate learning	STCA Coding	STCA Coding
Knowledge of alphabet	Index Filing Test	Index Filing test
English usage	STCA Language	-
Arithmetic	STCA Arithmetic	FIT Arithmetic
Vocational interest	Rothwell Interest Blank	-
Values/motivation	Survey of Interpersonal Values	Survey of Personal
Introversion-extraversion	-	Contact Personality Factor
Anxiety	-	Self-Analysis Form

in the lower two groups. All were female.

The sample was drawn by the investigator from nominal rolls with age and rating indicated. Although the stratified random sample was drawn appropriately, absences on the days of testing led to the slight imbalance in age and grading. Length of service was not used in selecting the sample but a check afterwards showed that in two locations the mean length of service for younger and older members was almost identical while in the other two the older people had had longer service. Length of service by grading was reasonably equal in one location. In the other three, the higher graded persons had had longer service.

CRITERION MEASURES

In concurrent validity studies as in predictive studies the nature of the criterion is critical.

In neither company was existing information really as useful as it needed to be. In the insurance company annual assessments could be misleading as a member of staff automatically received a minimum grade during her first 6-9 months in a new post - even though she might have had a maximum rating in the previous job. Each member was graded according to her progress through the hierarchy. These grades were used because obtaining a special rating would have placed too heavy demands on supervisors at that particular time.

In the mail order company the annual assessments, while not confounded in the same way, were not in a form that could be used in statistical analysis. In the mail order company both a general rating and special work-specific ratings were obtained. In this report the analysis using the general ratings only will be considered.

CONTRIBUTION OF EACH INDIVIDUAL TEST

This was established by computing phi coefficients for each test.

Ability and aptitude tests

For the ability and aptitude tests the coefficients which reached a statistically significant level are presented in Figure 8:2. The results of tests of personal characteristics are discussed separately.

In the insurance company, eight of the test scores correlated with the criterion, but no company would want to use eight scores or even the six tests from which they were obtained.

In the mail order company there were three tests which individually correlated with the ratings for the total group. However, inspection of Figure 8:2 shows that not all were equally effective in each of the four locations.

Figure 8.2 Correlation between test scores and performance

Ability	Insurance	Total	Mail order locations			
			A	B	C	D
Numerical ability	0.40					
Intelligence	0.26					
Accuracy of name checking	0.37					
Accuracy of checking names and numbers	0.30	0.31	0.36	–	–	0.34
Knowledge of alphabet	0.34					
Arithmetic	0.45	0.33	–	0.32	0.33	0.42
Immediate learning	0.24					
Verbal ability (PTI)	0.23	0.21	0.43	–	–	–
Size of sample	70	148	34	37	39	38
Minimum significant value acceptable	0.23	0.16	0.33	0.32	0.31	0.31

113

Measures of personal values
Very often personnel and line managers express the need for information about motivation, dependability and similar traits. In practice, however, they seldom have the necessary time nor do they have suitably trained staff to obtain this information. In concurrent validity studies when ample time is available (and time usually can be found) there is a strong case for including measures of this type. When this is done, the inclusion of such measures can indicate the contribution they could make to the selection process.

At the insurance company not quite enough time was available and so not everyone completed both measures of personal characteristics. The Survey of Interpersonal Values was completed by 43 graded staff. Only 17 persons completed the Survey of Personal Values so no results are presented.

The mean raw scores and mean percentiles for the high and low groups for interpersonal values are given in Figure 8:3.

Figure 8:3 Mean scores and percentile equivalents on Survey of Interpersonal Values for insurance sample

	Low group N=23		High group N=20	
	Mean	percentile	Mean	percentile
Support	17.9	45	17.0	34
Conformity	14.1	45	13.9	45
Recognition	8.9	24	8.5	24
Independence	18.5	65	18.8	65
Benevolence	20.0	54	20.0	54
Leadership	10.2	42	11.5	55

The mean percentile scores for high- and low-rated groups were almost identical for the six values. The absence of significant differences in the scores of the two groups indicates that in an insurance company interpersonal values do not relate to performance on the job. However, there is some interest in the order of importance of the six values for all members in the sample. These are benevolence (being helpful to other people), independence (having some opportunity to do things in one's own way), support (people being helpful and friendly towards one), conformity (doing what is expected of one), leadership (being in a position of authority), recognition (having people acknowledge what one has done). There is some interest in looking at the order for each of the groups. The most appropriate way of doing this is to consider the order of percentile ranks rather than the mean scores themselves. That being the case both groups attach most importance to being able to do things in their own way (something they probably cannot readily do in an insurance company). While both attach importance to being friendly and helpful to other people, the high-rated group considers it more important to be in a position of leadership (second for them and fifth for the low-rated group). Both groups agree that recognition is least important. The low-rated group consider it more important to have the support of other people than do the high group.

The number completing the Survey of Interpersonal Values was too small for the full analysis. However, inspection of mean scores of high and low groups indicates sizeable differences between them on four of the six values.

In the mail order company the Survey of Personal Values was used in three of the locations only, where 109 members participated. Mean scores, standard deviations and percentiles are given in Figure 8:4.

Figure 8:4 Mean scores and percentile equivalents on Survey of Personal Values for mail order sample

	Low group N=50			High group N=59		
	$\bar{X}$	s.d.	per-centile	$\bar{X}$	s.d.	per-centile
Practical-mindedness	15.3	3.6	74	17.3	4.9	84
Achievement	15.6	1.5	51	15.2	5.4	44
Variety	9.9	6.9	30	7.6	6.9	23
Decisiveness	15.6	2.1	58	14.9	6.2	52
Orderliness	15.7	6.8	64	16.2	3.8	64
Goal orientation	17.2	6.8	44	17.7	2.9	51

The mean scores are similar but the high-rated group attaches significantly more importance to doing things that pay off and they tend to value variety less.

When scores were related to ratings there was a significant correlation between practical-mindedness and overall rating, indicating that clerks who thought it was important to do things that paid off immediately were rated as more effective than those who did not. This finding was clearly replicated in one of the locations and tentatively in the others. In other locations a high score on variety was related to a poor performance rating. There was also a negative correlation between decisiveness and performance.

BEST COMBINATION OF TESTS

The next step was to estimate the combination of tests which would make the maximum contribution to the selection decision.

This step was carried out in two ways, first by totalling the scores of the individual tests having highest correlations with the criterion and second by running the full results through a stepwise regression program.

The first approach, while very effective, could at times be misleading in that two or more of the best single tests might be highly correlated with each other in which case they would together make a smaller contribution than if they did not correlate. The stepwise multiple regression analysis takes care of this problem. Such an analysis may suggest a combination of tests, not all of which individually necessarily correlate strongly with the criterion, but which do make a contribution when combined with other tests.

Another practical constraint to be considered at this stage was the request from each company that the test battery be as short as possible, certainly not more than half an hour and preferably less.

Insurance

Bearing in mind the time constraint and the similarity of numerical ability and arithmetic (0.78) and of PTI-V and TMA - verbal (0.70), it was decided to concentrate attention on four tests: STCA Arithmetic, STCA Coding, PTI-Verbal and Index Filing Test.

The multiple correlation of all four with the grading was 0.46, that of the three tests (Coding excluded) 0.44 and that of two tests (Filing excluded) 0.40. Using only the first part of the Arithmetic Test (four operations) the multiple correlation of 0.46 rises to 0.51 (adding other tests would have only increased the multiple correlation to 0.58).

A simpler way of representing the effectiveness of all or some of the four tests is in expectancy charts.

In Figure 8:5, which represents the usefulness of the PTI-Verbal and Arithmetic tests, it can be seen that of the people who obtained a composite score of 66, 64 per cent were grade 4 or 5 and only 36 per cent were grade 2 or 3. Looked at another way, of those people scoring 65 or less, 29 per cent were grade 4 or 5, while 71 per cent were grade 2 or 3.

Figure 8:5 Expectancy chart: PTI-Verbal and Arithmetic

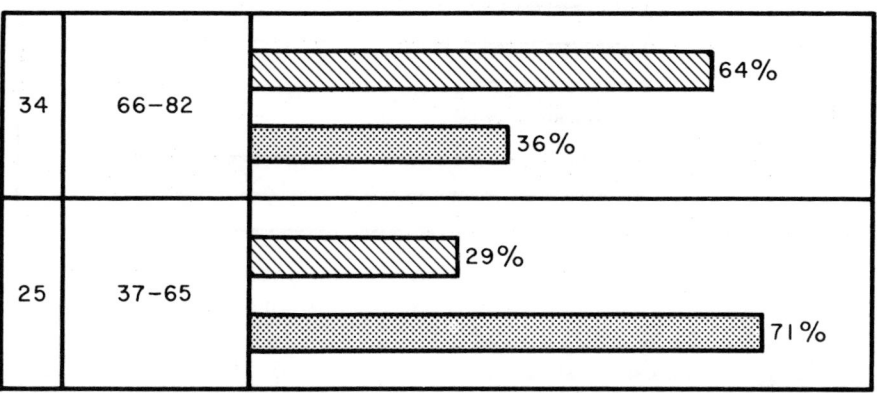

The expectancy chart summarizing the information about the three-test battery - PTI Verbal, Arithmetic and Filing - shows that 70 per cent and 30 per cent respectively (Figure 8:6) of grades 4 and 5 and grades 2 and 3 scored over 109, while those scoring below are 28 and 72 per cent respectively. The inclusion of the Coding Test increases the correlation and also slightly increases the percentage of people in grades 4 and 5 who score over the cutoff score of 185 (Figure 8:7).

Figure 8:6 Expectancy chart: PTI-Verbal, Arithmetic and Filing

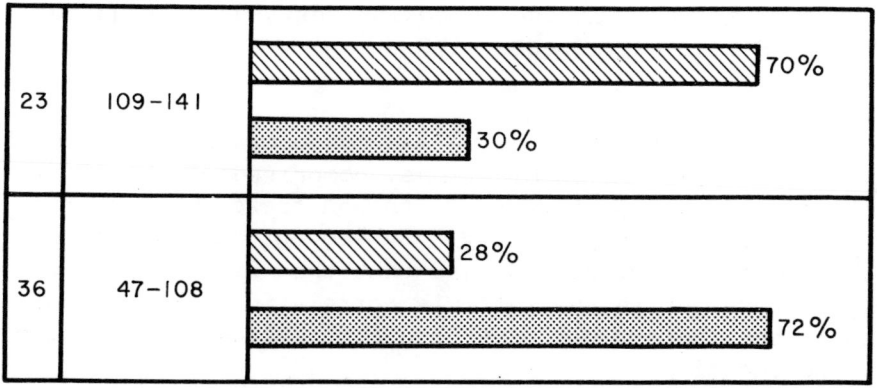

Considering these expectancy charts in relation to future recruitment - if on the four-test battery a cutoff of 185

Figure 8:7 Expectancy chart: PTI-Verbal, Arithmetic, Filing, Coding

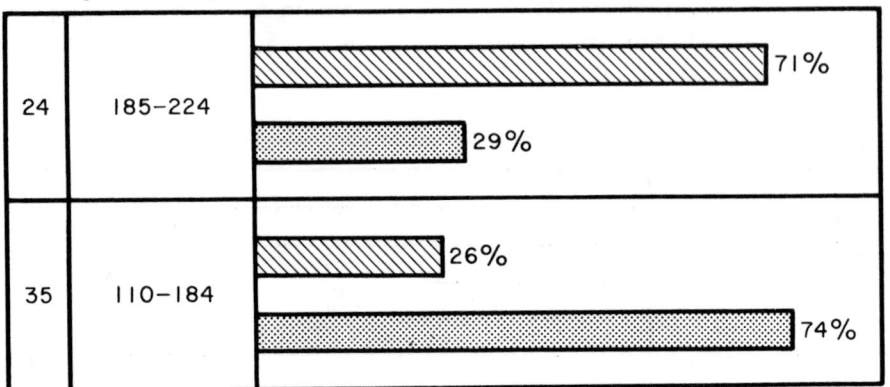

were taken, then there would be 71 chances in 100 that people appointed would be suitable for promotion eventually to grade 4 or 5 posts.

If only a three-test battery were used, then 70 per cent could be expected to be successful. In practice, it would be necessary to look very carefully at the other information about people scoring lower than 185 on the four-test battery or lower than 109 on a three-test battery before making an offer of employment.

In addition to considering the composite score, it would also be necessary to look at individuals to see that the test scores were not too low in any one case, for example, people scoring 20 or less on Arithmetic, 41 or less on Filing, 70 or less on Coding and 41 or less on PTI-Verbal.

Had there not been time restrictions, a somewhat more powerful combination would have been the Test of Mental Alertness and the Clerical Checking test, which require 25 and 18 minutes respectively.

Mail order
For this situation, attention was concentrated on the best two- and three-test combinations, comprised of the Clerical Checking and Arithmetic Tests and these two plus the PTI-Verbal Test respectively. Subsequent analysis of four tests (Coding included) showed that this did not lead to any improvement in the multiple correlation for the whole sample but there would have been some improvement in each of the locations.

Figure 8:8 gives phi values derived from total scores for two and three tests. The multiple correlations calculated by a computer were of the same order.

Figure 8:8 Phi values for the mail order sample

Locations	Two tests	Three tests
all	0.35	0.40
A	0.35	0.35
B	0.40	0.50
C	0.33	0.49
D	0.21	0.26

When expectancy charts similar to those shown for the previous example were prepared, it was seen that of the staff obtaining a composite score of 111 or more on the two tests, 68 per cent were in the high-rated group and 32 per cent in the low-rated group. For the three-test combination using a cutoff score of 141, 79 per cent of the high-rated group and 21 per cent of the low-rated group obtained scores above the cutoff.

Detailed analysis of the data for each location led to the suggestion of different cutoff scores for each. As well as the composite score recommendations, minimum scores on each test were suggested.

EFFECTIVENESS

Sun Alliance and London, which had entered into the exercise with a firm determination to implement the findings of the concurrent validity study, subsequently became involved in other managerial matters and had to defer the introduction of tests. In the year or so since the study was completed experience has shown its central personnel department that such tests would be very useful. At the time of going to press steps are being taken to introduce tests for clerical applicants throughout the group.

The mail order company introduced the tests immediately into two locations (A and B) and has been using them in a shadow fashion in two others (D and E) where the tests are given to all selected applicants on their first morning in the training school. Statistical analysis was recommended on the first 50 appointments to each location. The analysis to date is briefly summarized below.

In the other two locations (C and F) senior management decided against introducing the tests immediately as they felt the labour market was particularly poor at the time and would not provide an adequate test of the new procedure.

In location B, of 140 applicants, 86 were appointed.

Of these, 53 left before their training period of 6 weeks was completed. This suggested very strongly that in that location there were other, as yet unidentified, factors that needed attention. The mean scores of those who left and those who stayed were almost identical on each of the three tests. Dispersions of scores were also equal so it was not a case of appointing persons who were too able for the job. Nor did they differ on age.

In location A, 48 were accepted and 35 rejected. Of the 48 only 13 left before completion of training. At location A, the stayers and leavers did not differ on test scores or on age.

The assessment of training was done on a four-point rating scale and on a percentage score on an end-of-course test. For the purposes of the analysis a grade of 5 was given to people who did not complete training.

The correlation results are given in Figure 8:9.

Figure 8:9 Correlation between test scores and training grades

Location	A	B	D	F
N	33	53	41	28
PTI-V	0.04	0.28*	0.48**	0.25
ARITH.	0.51**	0.00	0.06	0.18
CLER.	0.25	0.46**	0.39**	0.46*
V+A+C	0.45**	0.62**	0.16	0.45*
A+C	0.61**	0.25	0.33*	0.42*
V+C	0.16	0.34*	0.47**	0.52**
A+V	0.20	0.30*	0.47**	0.17

*0.05 level of significance   **0.01 level of significance

In Figure 8:9 locations A, B and D are the same locations as participated in the concurrent validity study while E is a new one. Inspection of the table shows that the pattern from the previous concurrent validity study has not been replicated exactly, but there is evidence in each location that a single test or a combination of tests yielded a significant correlation, again indicating that the use of tests was helping to select people appropriate for the job. Overall, the better predictions are obtained by combining the clerical and arithmetic tests. In some cases the inclusion of the verbal test lowers the multiple correlation. The exception was in location E where the verbal intelligence test by itself had a higher correlation than any combination of tests. Here the combination of the clerical test and the verbal test is almost the same and it would therefore be recommended that the clerical test be included in the battery, in the interests of uniformity in the company.

Again the time factor prevented the scale of personal values being included in the basic selection battery. However, in order to gain further knowledge about the scale, location A administered the scale to the first 43 people who were appointed to the company. Of these, 26 completed training while 17 dropped out. The only value on which the people who stayed on the course differed from those who dropped out was orderliness, with those who dropped out considering orderliness to be more important for them than those who stayed. It was also the most important factor of the six for this group. The dropout group was slightly more decisive and slightly more oriented to long-term goals than the people who stayed.

When the trainees who were graded 1 and 2 (i.e. were very successful) were compared with those who were graded 3,4 or 5, the only factor on which the differences approached significance was achievement, the high-rated people attaching more importance to achievement than the low-rated people.

CONCLUSION

These two examples, taken from organizations with large clerical staffs, indicate that a relatively short test battery of two or three tests, taking no more than half an hour of testing time, can make a contribution to the selection of clerical staff. In the foregoing presentation no attempt has been made to evaluate or to specify the weight the company has placed on information gained from application forms or interview. It is also clear that factors other than selection can affect outcome, in particular reducing turnover. The identification of these factors and attention to them could well be given higher priority than the improvement of selection methods.

9

Use of Tests for Local Authority Staff

J. Gibson

DIFFICULTIES IN SELECTION PECULIAR TO LOCAL AUTHORITIES

Unlike commercial organizations, local authorities cannot use the yardstick of profitability when assessing the efficiency and effectiveness of their managerial and administrative staff. This is not such a serious difficulty as might at first appear, as in the large commercial organizations of today there are many members of managerial grades whose relationship to profitability is tenuous and whose success in work has to be judged by other means. However, if a mistake is made in selection in a commercial or industrial organization it is usually possible to rectify the mistake in one way or another, ultimately by discharging the manager concerned. In local authorities this is not so easy; the possibilities of transferring members of staff from one department to another are limited, and to discharge a member of staff is almost impossible unless he commits a serious breach of discipline. From this it follows that selection has to be correct in the first place because, if the wrong

---

The work on which this chapter is based was carried out in the former authorities of London County Council and the County Boroughs of Newcastle, Middlesbrough and Teesside.

selection is made, there is little chance of correcting it later and the wrongly selected person will remain on the staff of the local authority as long as he wishes. In the selection of senior and experienced administrative or professional staff these difficulties are supposed not to arise but there are well-authenticated accounts of failure to select wisely even in this field.

The principal difficulties in selection of staff for the local authority services stem from tradition and resistance to change. For many years the selection procedure pattern consisted of a more or less elaborate interview or series of interviews, once more or less relevant academic examinations had been passed. The local authorities' selection pattern was strongly influenced by that of the Civil Service. Little or no attempt was made to investigate the possibility that new methods of selection might be more effective, and indeed little attempt was made to investigate the effectiveness of the methods of selection already in use. In fact it is not too much to say that the question of the reliability and validity of the interview methods and of the examinations used for selection at that time was never seriously raised. This was partly due to inertia, a kind of passive acceptance of what had already been done, and partly due to a lack of knowledge that there were any other methods of selection which might be more effective. In this respect local authorities were not alone, but the more advanced organizations in business and industry were already forging ahead and using more modern methods.

It is in the less tradition-bound departments and fields of activity of local authorities that the more recently developed scientific methods of selection are employed. These methods are called scientific because, in them, every effort is made to avoid subjective impressions, prejudice and bias. Although only partial success in this endeavour has been achieved, it is a considerable advance on anything that has gone before. Such a relative freedom from bias is attainable by the use of psychological tests, but in the very novelty of achieving relative freedom from bias lies a challenge which has provoked the resistance of the more traditional thinkers. It is felt that there is something inhuman in the very process of weighing up a person's intelligence, special abilities and personality by means of figures and calculations.

DECISION TO USE TESTS

In local authorities the main factors influencing the introduction of tests were relative freedom from tradition, an open mind for the use of modern methods, and considerable doubt and uncertainty concerning the sufficiency of traditional methods for identifying the right candidates. Children's departments, and later social services departments, and also engineering departments, all faced with new and rapidly expanding demands for their services decided that they needed to call on outside resources to aid them in the selection of candidates. They saw that their most crucial limiting factors were the quantity and quality of staff, and that to get the best service from a limited number of employees it made sense to employ psychological testing to identify the most competent, effective and efficient workers. It was partly the novelty of the tasks set, bringing with it considerable uncertainty about the best method of selection, coupled with the knowledge of the greater sophistication and reliability of psychological tests today in comparison with what they were some years ago, which no doubt led these departments to decide to employ psychological testing as part of their selection procedure. Another factor influencing departmental heads in favour of the use of psychological tests was the obvious good sense and utility of the advice offered by psychologists quite apart from the specialist services which they were able to provide.

Feeling themselves faced with a selection situation rather different from those with which they had coped in the past, local authority departments turned to psychological methods for aid partly because they felt that these methods were sufficiently developed to be able to offer them what they wanted at this stage, but also for a purely fortuitous reason — that is to say, that they happened to have someone on their departmental staffs who knew sufficient about modern psychological methods to be able to indicate what they might be able to accomplish.

The final argument in favour of the employment of psychological tests as such, as distinct from other psychological methods, was the result of the experimental period, during which tests were used and at the end of which local authorities were satisfied that they were getting better information for selection purposes and for the planning of training than they had got by other methods previously. This is undoubtedly the most satisfactory criterion, particularly if it is backed up by data which, in the longer term, show that standards of selection have in fact improved.

PURPOSES FOR WHICH TESTS ARE USED

The purposes for which tests have been and are still being used are as follows:

1 Selection of staff, both qualified and unqualified
2 Appraisal and guidance of staff already in post
3 Providing advice to senior officers in the deployment and placing of staff
4 The identification of training needs
5 The provision of information for training officers and supervisors for use during the training period, indicating the requirements of each particular employee.

The difference between purposes 4 and 5 may require explanation. Purpose 4 is concerned with identifying what may reasonably be called the weaknesses of each employee; that is, the needs and deficiencies which the training should supply. Purpose 5 is concerned also with the strengths of the employee; that is to say, he may understand or respond to training better in one way than in another, and it is advisable that training officers and supervisors should be aware of this. Purpose 5 is also concerned with the interests and motivation of employees, in so far as knowledge of these areas may be used to help them to find their place in the organization.

STAFF ASSESSED BY TESTS

Psychological testing has been used as part of an assessment (including selection) procedure for a wide range of staff, which may be classified as follows:

1 Higher management level, including chief officers, deputies and assistant chief officers
2 Middle management levels, including senior administrative staff
3 Supervisory staff
4 Professional staff
5 Social case workers and residential staff
6 Junior staff

Tests were used for different purposes in each of the above categories; details are given in Figure 9:1.

Figure 9:1 *Purposes for which tests are used by local authorities*

	Categories of staff	Selection 1	Appraisal 2	Advice 3	Training needs 4	Information for training officers 5
1	Higher management		X	X		
2	Middle management	X	X	X	X	
3	Supervising	X	X	X	X	X
4	Professional	X		X	X	X
5	Social case workers and resident staff	X	X	X	X	X
6	Junior	X		X	X	X

126

THE TESTS AND THEIR CONTRIBUTION

Tests used
The tests used were the following:

1 Sixteen Personality Factor Questionnaire, forms A, B, and C
2 Eysenck Personality Inventory
3 Tests supplied by the NIIP (general and speical ability)
4 Moray House Adult Intelligence Test 1
5 Attitude measures.

Evaluation of the contribution made by tests
The evaluation of the contribution made by tests is a complex matter, and should not be confused with the statistical validation of the tests or a measurement of their reliability, essential as these procedures are. The evaluation of the contribution made by a test must also cover the help which the test results give to interviewers in prompting new questions which they would not have thought of without having the test results before them, as well as the additional information provided directly by the test results. The statistical aspects are set out in Figure 9:2, but we are here concerned with the wider context of how far officers responsible for selection, appraisal, placement, training and supervision find that the additonal information provided by test results helps them in making their decisions.

It has been found in every case that responsible officers welcome the access of additional information, because they are acutely conscious of the fact that they are required to make decisions which may affect the lives of their staff quite widely and may affect the efficiency and effectiveness of their organization without having adequate information in front of them in many cases. In these circumstances the additional information provided by tests is felt by them to be a real contribution to decision-making. It is clearly the responsibility of the psychologist to point out to these officers the limitations of test results and in particular that there is no such thing as perfect reliability and perfect validity. Provided a client understands the limitations within which he is working, he not unreasonably feels that the more information he has to guide him the better. In fact, this is the faith behind all scientific endeavour: although it may be possible from time to time to find instances in which better decisions were made on the basis of inadequate and faulty information, it is necessary to proceed on the basis that the more information that can be fed into the decision-making process the better it is likely to be, provided the information is the best available in the circumstances.

Much criticism of tests is predicated on the basis that they are not perfect, but in many situations in which the decision is of some importance it is impossible to do without their contribution unless something that is better is put in their place. If it is argued that the sensitive evaluation of an employee or candidate by an experienced and trained interviewer is of more value than the results provided by tests then of course this evaluation by such an interviewer can be retained: the point is that the test results are additional to any valuable insights that may be produced, and few experienced and sensitive interviewers have such confidence in their own relative infallibity that they are prepared to dispense with the amount of information which can be provided by tests of the kind indicated above.

Sixteen Personality Factor Questionnaire

The many validation studies which have been carried out in connection with this test must be borne in mind, in spite of the severe criticisms which have been made of it. The criticisms, if they are based on empirical or experimental findings, indicate that there are occasions when we have to treat the results of this test with caution, but, in the practical situation, provided further information is brought in, either from other tests or from other sources to provide a cross-check, there is little danger of being misled. For this reason it is our general practice to use this test as one of a battery of tests which also includes the Eysenck Personality Inventory. In this way we get a satisfactory cross-check and our experience in general shows that we are likely to receive adequate warning if any of the components of the battery are sounding a false note.

Whenever possible we use form A or form B, or both if time is sufficient, but very often we use form C. One advantage of using form C is that it contains a motivation distortion scale which, in combination with the L scale on the Eysenck Personality Inventory, gives us a fairly good idea of whether the candidate is distorting for social desirability or not. This advantage is absent from forms A and B, but the disadvantage of form C is clearly that it is rather short to provide sufficient

Figure 9:2 Tests used by local authorities

	Categories of staff	16PF	EPI	Intelligence tests	Attitude tests	N	Percentage evaluations of tests as useful for purposes indicated in Figure 9:1
1	Higher management	42	42			42	98
2	Middle management	164	164	80		244	99
3	Supervising	238	238	238	347	585	90
4	Professional	152	152	152		152	98
5	Social case workers and resident staff	454	454	454		454	98
6	Junior	193	193	193		193	97

reliability. This is why it is important, whenever form C is used, to ensure that other adequate cross-checks are provided. Similarly if form A or form B is used without a motivation distortion scale it is important that the Eysenck Personality Inventory be included for the sake of the L scale, if for nothing else. In fact, the E and N scales of the Eysenck Personality Inventory provide a valuable cross-check of the sixteen personality factor questionnaire. The other factors of this test provide a wide coverage, but if form C is used it is better if at all possible to check on it by using form A or B.*

On the other hand if the client is not prepared to provide the time for using any form other than form C, that does not seem to be an adequate reason why he should be deprived of the indications that form C can give, provided he is warned of the risks that he may be running. In case of doubt some clients are prepared to test candidates again, and, in any case, if they feel the risks are too great they can discount the test results appropriately.

Eysenck Personality Inventory
This is one of the best researched and best validated instruments in personality assessment in the UK, and it has been reported on again and again in the journals and in other publications. When a personality assessment is required, it is impossible to exaggerate the importance of getting a reading on this instrument, particularly in view of the vast amount of information which has been gathered of the relationship between the factors E and N and occupational performance. This information is particularly valuable, because, in the Sixteen Personality Factor Questionnaire, until very recently, all the occupational information has been based upon American occupations and upon American norms, and is therefore hardly comparable with British circumstances.

The Eysenck Personality Inventory provides a wide range of British occupational information on the basis of British norms. In the volume of readings relating to fields of application of the Eysenck Personality Inventory (Eysenck 1971), the relationship between factor E and general adjustment to the job situation finds supporting evidence. There is no need to stress the importance of general adjustment to the job situation, and, if the likelihood of this general adjustment being achieved by an employee can be predicted from tests

*Or form D. (Editor.)

before employment, this is a considerable gain from the point of view of selection and later of placement. In the same volume the relation of temperament to vocational interests is considered, and carefully quantified by the use of Eysenck's factors E and N and of the Strong Vocational Interest Blank. Although this research carried out by Bendig in 1963 is based on American data, the results bear a predictable relationship with Eysenck's own work, which therefore gains support.

NIIP tests

The tests developed by the National Institute of Industrial psychology (and now distributed by NFER) constitute a battery covering a wide range of general and special abilities, or, to put it in more technical language which is somewhat dated, group factors of wider or narrower scope. This battery is particularly useful for occupational purposes and especially for selection and placement. No attempt is made to produce a test which predicts success in any particular job but, provided a job is correctly analysed and the abilities which it demands correctly identified, it is possible to use this battery to measure the extent to which a candidate for employment or a trainee is showing the relevant abilities. The word 'showing' is important, particularly in these tests of intelligence and special abilities: it is easy to show less than we have to show, but almost impossible to show more. It follows that if a person is showing a low score on ability tests but, on other grounds, it is believed the score should be considerably higher then there may be some other reason than lack of ability for the low score. This other reason is probably lack of motivation, but again more evidence is needed to confirm this possibility. In this way tests of general and special abilities, when combined with other evidence, can throw light on possible variations in motivation. But there is a problem here: it is the problem of combining different scores into one complete picture.

Campbell *et al.* (1970) cite many studies which concur in showing that the mechanical mode of data combination is superior to any other mode including the pure clinical mode of data combination and also a combined clinical and mechanical mode. What this appears to mean is that a weighted average of test results (provided the weights are correct) is superior to an intuitive judgment. But, it may be asked, how are we to assess the correct weights, except by an intuitive judgment? The answer is clearly that the weights need to be estimated by a statistical procedure, which can be found in any elementary textbook of statistics relating to the behavioural sciences. But another difficulty arises here, which is that the tests mentioned hitherto have not been designed on a sufficiently similar basis to allow their results to be combined in a simple weighted average. Furthermore, many organizations employ or deal with only small numbers of people at one time, which makes the statistical approach extremely difficult, if not impossible. It may well be, therefore, that only the clinical (individualistic) approach to data combination is feasible.

There is often, in any given organization, plenty of room for improvement in the clinical approach to combining test data into one picture. The word 'clinical' here refers to the attempt by interviewers and assessors to see each part of the picture revealed to them by tests as part of a general jigsaw puzzle, which will give them when fitted together a complete picture of the candidate - a kind of identikit which can be used for purposes of prediction.

Moray House Adult Intelligence Test 1
This has been found useful as an alternative intelligence test to the NIIP battery for young adults.

Summary
The contribution of tests to selection, appraisal and guidance, the identification of training needs, and the provision of a basis for wider advice and information to senior and training staff has been encouraging, whether viewed from the point of view of statistical evaluation or from the clinical standpoint. Tests are generally regarded primarily as instruments for providing answers to questions. They do fulfil this function of course, but they also fulfil another function: of prompting questions in the minds of interviewers and senior officers which they would not otherwise have thought of. They have been found particularly useful in providing information and suggestions for training officers. In fact, it can be said that the proper use of test results not only provides an ending to one series of questions, investigations and problems, but it also provides a beginning and, it is hoped, a more fruitful beginning than would otherwise be possible, to a new endeavour to help the new employees, trainees and established staff to attain their objectives.

FUTURE DEVELOPMENTS

From what has already been said, it is clear that there is a need for a new battery of tests covering general abilities, a wide range of special abilities, personality and motivation, designed in such a way that the test results can be integrated into an overall picture of the candidate or of the person being assessed without recourse to clinical intuition more than is absolutely necessary. In this way it will be possible to minimize the dangers of subjective distortion of the data, but clearly there is a long way to go before such a possibility is even in sight. It is clearly neither an attainable nor a desirable objective to dispense with clinical or intuitive judgment entirely, but it is necessary to control such judgment by constant recourse to the observed facts and to statistical analysis and inference. Hence the first priority is to develop a battery of tests which can be integrated statistically, and preferably by computer, covering the fields of intelligence and abilities, personality and what used to be called character, and motivation.

Perhaps it is not too much to hope also for a better understanding by the general public of the objectives, achievements and difficulties of testing. As a community we aim at the best use of our resources, both material and human, and testing makes a modest contribution towards this objective. Achievements have, on the whole, exceeded expectations, especially in the area of ability testing: those who expected infallibility have, of course, been disappointed. But there are many problems still to be solved, many improvements still to be carried out, and a great deal of research is still needed. One important practical problem, to which a good deal of attention should be given in the near future, is the question of how best to separate temporary influences from more enduring tendencies in human behaviour as observed in everyday performance, surveys and testing situations. Yet another problem is to reflect accurately the differences between the sexes, and between cultures and subcultures. All positions are now open to people of all cultures, and in the very near future there will be complete equality between the sexes in their eligibility for jobs, so that selectors will have an even more difficult task in the future than they have today in selecting from among the candidates who present themselves.

Above all, new measures of personality traits and of

motivation are required. It is sometimes asserted, in a somewhat extreme way, that personality traits do not exist, or, if they do, that they make only a minimal contribution to occupational behaviour. The objection that something does not exist is not a sufficient reason for not using it: the equator does not exist, but it is a very useful thing to use. Inches and feet do not exist apart from the objects which they are used to measure. So it is misleading to say that personality traits do not exist apart from the situations in which they are manifested, as if this implied that they did not constitute a useful means of measurement. In fact, there is no real alternative. When a selection between people has to be made for a given position, the decision-maker has to ask himself questions of the following form. In situations A, B and/or C, which are known to arise in the given position, is candidate X likely to be more cooperative and outgoing to people, more controlled emotionally, more approachable, more persevering, more prepared to take a risk, more cautious, more sensitive, more imaginative, more relaxed or tense, more anxious or more self-reliant than candidate Y? Such questions would not have to be asked, of course, unless candidates X and Y were virtually equal in other relevant respects. But, given that the candidates are equally well qualified in other respects, it is precisely on grounds such as these that the final selection is made in many cases, unless the selector is so biased that he selects on the basis of personal liking. In parentheses, it may be said that personal liking is a relevant basis for the selection of a secretary or colleague who has to work very closely with a particular executive: in such cases personal compatibility is an important consideration. But, in other cases, selectors have to consider the personal qualities of the candidate which may be called his personality.

There are only two choices here: one is to carry out the selection with regard to personality systematically and with due regard to all the variables concerned, the other is to carry it out unsystematically and by guess. Probably the best information in this difficult area is contained in a person's track record or recent performance, but this is frequently inaccessible and, in the case of young people, virtually nonexistent or very meagre. Another point that, unfortunately, has to be considered, is that a substantial number of people, after years of good performance, suffer from severe deterioration or at least from noticeable instability, and here tests can help both the organization and the candidate by ensuring that extra responsibilities are not placed upon a person who is unable to carry them.

If psychological tests are to be used to their full potential, it is essential that responsible officers in organizations employing them should understand that sufficient time must be given for the information which can be gathered by the tests to be assembled, processed, checked and interpreted. It is important that it should become an accepted thing that all these processes should take place over a period of time, because psychological tests cannot possibly yield all the information they are capable of providing if they are used in a short, machine-gun like burst, on the basis of which reliable reports are supposed to be prepared by the unfortunate psychologist.

It is probably not too much to hope for the future that local authorities, which use the most modern methods of computing, accounting, statistical processing and engineering, will also lead the way in developing and using the best methods of personnel selection and appraisal. The combination, in appropriate circumstances, of well-designed and recently standardized tests with sensitive interviewing will lead, not only to an improvement in the local authority services and staffing, but also to a general advance in the related techniques of personnel management. This is a development to which we may confidently look forward, and which is already commencing in this and in other western countries.

REFERENCES

Campbell, J.P., Dunnette, M.D., Lawler, E.E. & Weick, K.E. (1970), *Managerial Behavior, Performance and Effectiveness* (New York: McGraw-Hill)

Eysenck, H.J. (ed.)(1971), *Readings in Extraversion-Introversion*, vol.2, 'Fields of application' (London: Staples Press)

10

Use of Tests in a National Retail Company

R. Beaton

Telefusion Limited is a national television rental and retail company with 350 outlets, 80 service departments, and employing approximately 3500 staff. The use of tests has to be considered against this background in the retailing industry, which has for many years suffered from a poor image for employment. The general impression is that workers in retailing have low wages and uncongenial hours, particularly Saturday working and this image is still fostered by many careers masters. The industry itself has accepted the image without really fighting it, and has adopted unprofessional attitudes to general recruitment and selection techniques. Those few companies that have taken a professional approach are household names, and stand head and shoulders above their rivals.

FACTORS INFLUENCING THE INTRODUCTION OF TESTS

Moreover, many managers in retailing, though possessing many qualities making for success, are lacking in formal management education, and are essentially practical people who have worked their way up through the organization with a resulting suspicion of sophisticated techniques. Applicants themselves do not expect to meet professional interviewing standards, let alone selection tests.

Finally, because of the geographical spread of a national retailing operation, the selection decisions have to be made at a comparatively low level in the structure.

These factors caused us to undertake the education and training of our managerial staff in general selection and interviewing techniques, before we could consider using tests.

Additionally we had to consider the general problems in introducing selection tests into any company, namely the cost in time and money. By definition, in order to establish predictive validity, there must be a considerable time lag and we felt that in most of the categories discussed below one year had to lapse between testing and applying the criterial if a person's true performance was to be properly validated. Also, of course, a lot of the time and money which a personnel department spends on trying out tests will be wasted as many of the tests will not turn out to have any worthwhile validity. Failures have to be expected along with the successes.

OBJECTIVES

In the light of the above, our objectives in introducing testing were as follows:

1 To improve overall selection standards and attitudes. Tests formed a focal point, and served as a means of drawing attention to the benefits to be gained from a professional overall selection system.
2 To create the impression amongst potential applicants who would very likely come from within the television rental industry that Telefusion was not an easy company to gain a position with, and therefore people without the necessary qualifications should not apply. In a word, to reduce the quantity and to increase the quality of applicants.
3 To present the results of the tests in a way that could be utilized and understood by local managers. This thought will be amplified later.
4 In some categories our turnover was very high, as is common in the industry, and we were particularly concerned to find people who would stay with us and do a competent job.
5 In other categories the training period was very long with a consequently high cost so that accurate selection was vital.
6 In other categories there was a great shortage of staff,

particularly skilled television engineers, and we were therefore concerned with the identification of potential.

SITUATIONS IN WHICH ONE TYPE OF CRITERION ONLY WAS SUITABLE

We did a great deal of work with trainee engineers, who were recruited from an unskilled background and were put through a training course consisting of on-the-job classroom and workshop instruction lasting 28 weeks. The amount of production that they contributed during that period was minimal. The cost of training each individual was calculated at £1000 and therefore failures were expensive. In an attempt to find the best statistical method of extracting information from tests that were applied and the best methods of presenting the results to line management, several approaches were used.

Group 1

A battery of three tests was applied to group 1. These tests were the AH4, the ACER Mechanical Reasoning and the Revised Minnesota Paper Form Board Tests. The criterion was the score on the Engineering Trade Test (an objective, multiple-choice test of the practical aspects of diagnosing faults in television sets) applied six weeks after completion of the course.

These tests were used as the basis for expectancy charts. In order to ensure statistical accuracy the formula compiled by Lawshe was used as this includes a double correlation significance check (phi correlation and chi-squared).

A scattergram was drawn for each of the three tests against the grading results. The first two, AH4 and Mechanical Reasoning, showed a general correlation. However, in both cases the scattergram was shaped somewhat like a fan with the wide end to the bottom left corner. In other words the tests predicted well for high scorers but not for low scorers in that it was clear that those who scored high on the test would score high on the grading, but those who scored poorly on the test could score either poorly or well on the grading. The third test was not used as no general correlation was found.

The phi coefficient for the AH4 expectancy chart was 0.45 and for the ACER Mechanical 0.55, and the significance checks proved positive. Results for both expectancy charts are indicated in Figure 10:1 where both individual charts and institutional charts are shown.

Figure 10:1 Expectancy charts for AH4 and ACER Mechanical Reasoning Tests indicating percentage chances of passing Trade Test for group 1 (technical trainees)

AH4

	Individual	Institutional
Score		
48-49	75	75
37-47	62	68
32-36	50	62
25-31	38	56
15-25	23	50

ACER Mech.

	Individual	Institutional
Score		
20-23	72	72
17-19	53	62
15-16	38	54
14	26	47
7-13	12	40

The individual chart indicates the chances of a person in that range of scores being rated superior. The institutional chart indicates the percentage of applicants who would be rated superior if all applicants with minimum scores in each range were selected. These have the advantage of being easily explained to the managers; for example, an individual with a score on the AH4 of 48 or 49 has very nearly 8 chances out of 10 of passing the Trade Test, while one with a score of 15-25 has only a 1 in 5 chance. Equally, it can be explained that if everyone with a score of 15 or more is taken then only half will pass.

Group 2
The second group of trainees was selected on the basis of these charts and the predictions proved remarkably accurate. Indicated in Figure 10:2 is the percentage predicted superior by each institutional chart, together with the percentage that was actually superior in the event from this second group.
  However, in indicating how successful an individual could be, this procedure has some drawbacks. First, it is

difficult to combine the results of two or more tests in any statistical sense. Having established some relationship between the tests and the results, we felt that we could compile a double expectancy table for groups 1 and 2 combined, the results of which are given in Figure 10:3.

Figure 10:2 Actual and predicted results achieved by group 2 (technical trainees) in Trade Test

	Percentage predicted passing Trade Test from AH4 institutional expectancy chart	Percentage actually successful
48-49	75	100
37-47	68	70
32-36	62	62
25-31	56	54
15-25	50	53

N = 32

	Percentage predicted passing Trade Test from ACER mechanical institutional expectancy chart	Percentage actually successful
20-23	72	55
17-19	62	62
15-16	54	55
14	47	57
7-14	40	47

N = 32

This produced some results that one would expect, namely that a combination of high scores gave an exceptionally high chance of being rated superior. But mainly it confirmed the indications of the scattergram that people scoring low on either of the tests could still pass the Trade Test. For example, of the 24 who were rated low on the ACER Mecanical Test, 10 passed and of the 25 who were rated low on the AH4 Test, 11 passed. Moreover, of the 33 in the 'lowest' boxes, A2/B3, A3/B3 and A3/B2, 17 passed. Again this can be discussed clearly with line managers and practical decisons made.

This whole procedure demonstrates the necessity of examining the relationship between the test scores and the criterion across the whole range of scores rather than relying on a global correlation coefficient which can cover up the differences in relationship in different parts of the score ranges.

Figure 10:3 Relationship between AH4, Mechanical Reasoning Test and pass or fail in Trade Test for groups 1 and 2 combined (technical trainees)

	B3	B2	B1	Totals		
A1	0	3	10	A1	C1	13
	1	1	1	A1	C2	3
A2	4	0	6	A2	C1	10
	5	6	2	A2	C2	13
A3	6	7	1	A3	C1	14
	8	3	0	A3	C2	11

Totals	B3 C1 10	B2 C1 10	B1 C1 17	N = 64
	B3 C2 14	B2 C2 10	B1 C2 3	

A1 = AH4 scores 38-45   B1 = ACER Mechanical scores 18-23
A2 = AH4 scores 37-37   B2 = ACER Mechanical scores 15-17
A3 = AH4 scores 15-26   B3 = ACER Mechanical scores 7-14

C1 = Pass Trade Test
C2 = Fail Trade Test

parts of the score ranges.

SITUATIONS IN WHICH THE ONE CRITERION WAS NOT CATEGORICAL BUT CONTINUOUS

The other major drawback with using this type of approach was that the criterion discriminates only two classes - pass or fail - and this represented perhaps too coarse a distinction. In this particular example, in the real situation, we did not dismiss people who failed the Trade Test as they were still of some use to us although not as much use as people who passed with a high mark. Clearly the real measurement of their abilities was a continuous measurement and not a categorical measurement. We felt, therefore, that it was necessary to predict results or marks in the grading test on a continuous scale. The only way in which this can be done is by regression and, while we could have computed manually regression equations for each of the tests and predicted Trade Test scores for each of the tests, it was felt that if we were going to do this we should combine the tests and produce a multiple correlation. For this purpose, computer assistance is necessary. This was obtained from Chorley College of Education.

All three tests were combined for group 1 and a multiple regression equation was obtained for the predicted Trade Test score = 0.3(ACER Mech.) + 1.1(AH4) + 0.2 (RMPFB) + 39.

In addition, it was felt that we should be concerned with two principal ratios: first the pass rate, that is the percentage of people selected with certain scores on the Test that would in the event pass - this, of course, is what the institutional expectancy charts do; second, a selection efficiency ratio, that is the percentage of the potentially successful applicants in the total group who were actually selected by the tests. The benefit of the layout in Figure 10:4 is that the pass rate, the selection efficiency and the predicted scores are all on one chart and, of course, they are worked out with all the tests working together with the best weighting. Pass rate and selection efficiency have been worked out on a specific score 75 as a pass, but can easily be recalculated for other pass marks.

These ratios are particularly useful in determining cut-off points, for example using a cut-off predicted score of 80, there would be 11 appointments of whom 9 would actually pass, giving a pass rate of 82%. However, in the total group of applicants there were 15 who were potentially successful of whom only 9 would be appointed at the same cut-off score of 80 giving a selection efficiency of 60%. Clearly, therefore, the greater number appointed out of a group of applicants, the higher will be the selection efficiency in that all potential successful applicants are captured, but the lower the pass rate in that more failures are appointed as well. Therefore, the

Figure 10:4 Technical trainees

Predicted score	Criterion score Pass	Criterion score Fail	Total number Passing	Total number Selected	Pass rate	Selection efficiency
90	90		1	1	100	7
88	92		2	2	100	13
86	82	74	3	4	75	20
85	90		4	5	80	27
83	94 85		6	7	86	40
82	83		7	8	87	47
81	83		8	9	89	53
80	78	68	9	11	82	60
79		74	9	12	75	60
78	96		10	13	77	67
77	84		11	14	79	73
75		74 62	11	16	69	73
74	84		12	17	71	80
73		52	12	18	67	80
71	84	72 72	13	21	62	87
70	80	74 37	14	24	58	93
68		60	14	25	56	93
67	92	64 62 53	15	29	52	100
64		70 70	15	31	48	100

test results do not make the selector's decision for him, but give him information on which to make his final judgment. This in turn, of course, is affected by other factors, for example, the number that need to be appointed. If 11 applicants had to be appointed then the selector would probably be happy with the pass rate of 82%. On the other hand if 24 positions had to be filled, the selector might not be happy with a pass rate of 58% and may seek to obtain a further group of applications. The decision really turns on how many passes are required and the number of fails then can be tolerated.

As group 2 had not taken the third test, the RMPFB, a simplified formula for the first two tests of ½AH4 + ACER Mechanical = predicted score was used. Of the 17 who were predicted to fail 6 actually passed. Of the 15 predicted to pass 1 actually failed. (The pass mark was set artificially high, at 75, to differentiate the top technicians, so that some trainees who 'failed' could still be considered competent).

SITUATIONS IN WHICH MORE THAN ONE TYPE OF CRITERION IS APPLIED

In some other types of situations continuous measures are not appropriate, particularly when more than one type of criterion is to be applied, and a different approach using simply raw data to produce expectancy tables might be preferred. Expectancy tables are easier to work with and a computer is not necessary. Also, the data may be manipulated more easily to bring out the combinations that have some meaning in relationship to several criteria.

This is quite a common situation because, fundamentally, selection is concerned with predicting whether an applicant will do at least two things:

1 Learn to perform the job to required standard.
2 Continue in the company's employment for a reasonable period of time.

We have tried this approach with our branch managers and salesmen who, during a one-month probation period, attend a course at our training centre. First, we applied the PTI-Verbal Test, which is a short, general ability verbal test, and categorized them according to Figure 10:5. Staying with the company was defined as staying for one year or more. As the numbers were small, group A was ignored for any significance test, but the chi-squared test was applied to groups B and C combined and group D. The result was a chi-squared of 14.031 which is significant at the 1 per cent level.

A check between groups B and C to see whether, as their chances of staying were the same, their sales performance could be differentiated, produced a chi-squared of 2.710 which was not significant, so it was felt better to use the combined chart and also to take service of one year or more as 'success' particularly as most of the 'low' sales were still acceptable to the company.

Figure 10:5 Relationship between PTI-V scores and performance for sales staff

Group	Scores	Total N	Leaving	Low sales	High sales
A	0-20	3	3	–	–
B	20-30	10	2	7	1
C	30-40	18	3	8	7
D	40 +	11	9	2	–
Totals		42	17	17	8

Raw data expectancy chart

Scores	Approximate odds of staying	Approximate odds of staying with high sales	Approximate odds of staying with low sales
A 0-20	0 out of 10	0 out of 10	0 out of 10
B 20-30	8 out of 10	1 out of 10	7 out of 10
C 30-40	8 out of 10	4 out of 10	3½ out of 10
D 40 +	2 out of 10	0 out of 10	2 out of 10

Raw data combined expectancy chart

Group	Score	Leaving	Staying	Total
B + C	20-40	5	23	28
D	40 +	9	2	11

Combined percentage chances of staying

Group scale	Approximate odds of staying
B+C 20-40	8 out of 10
D 40 +	2 out of 10

SITUATIONS IN WHICH PERSONALITY IS 'SUITED' TO A JOB

Cattell has outlined two approaches to deciding a person's suitability for a specific occupation or a particular job.

First is the effectiveness estimate approach in which goodness of performance is estimated by a quantitive value.

Second is the adjustment approach whereby a person is allocated to a specific group — for example a group of 'successful' salesmen. This is usually done by computing a similarity coefficient relating that person's profile to the mean profile of that group.

The first approach assumes a linear relationship between the various factors and the criterion, and is usually expressed as a linear regression equation with weights attaching to each factor.

The second approach assumes a curvilinear relationship as there is an 'optimum' value for each factor, that 'optimum' value being the mean score of the successful group in that factor.

We have 16PF data on 40 branch managers who were rated as successful or unsuccessful by a combination of sales results, administrative performance and managerial rating. As Cattell himself points out the relationship of some factors would be linear and of others curvilinear so a combination approach was tried out on the data, and it was found that there existed a negative linear relationship between factors E and L and the criterion and a curvilinear one between C, G and Q3 and the criterion. S, a selector indicator, was computed simply as E + L, being an approximation to a regression type of formula for the predicted criterion in terms of E and L (in fact, the higher the indicator the less suitable the person). Similarly a coefficient indicator $D^2 = (C - 6)^2 + (G - 5)^2 + (Q3 - 6)^2$ indicated degree of adjustment to the profile of a successful manager — again the lower the indicator the more suitable the person in terms of being closer to the 'optimum' values.

A combination of the two seemed to offer the best chances of prediction. Noted in Figure 10:6 are the selection efficiencies and rejection efficiencies for various combinations of the two predictors. The rejection efficiency is a new concept and is the ratio of failures rejected to total failures in whole group. This ratio is independent of the pass rate which depends on the percentages of

Figure 10:6 Efficiencies of various criteria for selecting branch managers

Criteria for selection			Predicted Selection efficiency	Predicted Rejection efficiency
S < 15			97.4	28.4
S < 13			82.8	61.0
		$D^2 < 25$	97.5	26.1
		$D^2 < 16$	87.2	51.2
S < 13	&	$D^2 < 16$	72.2	81.0
S < 15	&	$D^2 < 16$	85.0	65.1
S < 13	&	$D^2 < 25$	80.5	71.2
S < 15	&	$D^2 < 25$	95.0	47.1
S < 13	or	$D^2 < 16$	97.8	31.2

successes in the group used for analysis which might be misleadingly high. The rejection efficiency is therefore useful to use alongside the selection efficiency.

CONTRIBUTION OF TESTS TO TELEFUSION'S SELECTION PROCEDURE

The validation exercises described above have proved successful and useful, but we have also spent considerable time on exercises which provided us with no useful information so that failures have to be expected.

Even where tests prove valuable they can only be part of any selection procedure and no substitute for one. Telefusion's approach to selection is to use the 'multiple' approach similar to that used in assessment centres, in other words to use as many methods of selection as is feasible including tests and interviews and for these measures to be evaluated by several assessors. With this philosophy the tests described above can make a major contribution.

Part Three

Survey of the Use of Psychological Tests

11

The Use of Tests in British Industry and Commerce

Kenneth M. Miller

So far as can be ascertained, psychological tests were first used in British industry in 1924. The interest in psychological tests in industry and applied settings began in the late nineteenth century, arising from the work of Galton and James McKeen Cattell. The main stimulus to the use of tests in Britain came with the setting up of the National Institute of Industrial Psychology in 1921. The Institute staff carried out research into various psychological aptitudes and abilities, e.g. the work of Cox on mechanical aptitudes. It also initiated a programme of test development and the training of personnel staff in the use of tests. In the thirties, the Industrial Health and Fatigue Research Board also stimulated interest in areas such as manual dexterity.

In 1943 the National Foundation for Educational Research Test Agency was established. Initially, its concern was with the importation and distribution of tests for educational psychologists. Its activities soon expanded to include the distribution of American and Australian tests suitable for use in personnel work and later the publication of a few British tests. Several agencies have subsequently been started.

Very recently, two of the main American test publishers (Science Research Associates and Harcourt Brace Jovanovich) have commenced direct distribution from British subsidiaries. These publishers are also undertaking a programme of adaptation and standardization of their tests in the UK.

The increase in the availability of tests would seem to indicate an increasing use of tests. However, no information about the use of tests in practice had been gathered until, in 1963, the British Institute of Management carried out a survey of the use of all types of selection procedures by a sample of its member firms.

In 1964 the course organiser of the Institute of Personnel Management scheduled the first selection course which was attended by 21 members. Over 400 members have now been trained on subsequent courses. Course members were also interested to know how extensively tests were being used, so it was suggested to the IPM Research Committee that a survey be conducted among the Institute members. Some committee members were more than a little sceptical that there would be sufficient replies to such a survey to justify its analysis. However, in due course the Institute gave its blessing and a short questionnaire was developed and sent to all members with the Digest of March 1968 and redistributed with the July issue. The Institute met the costs of distribution, printing and part of the costs of the analysis. The Central Training Council made a contribution to the analysis in return for a special report.

The full report was printed and made available to IPM members and others in 1971. However, as the questions are still being asked and the report to date has had limited circulation, the main findings are being summarized in the present volume.

DESCRIPTION OF THE SAMPLE

At the time of the survey, the Institute of Personnel Management had approximately 8000 members in the UK. Completed questionnaires were returned by 842 members employed in 696 firms and organizations. As a check on representativeness, respondents were categorized according to the 24 orders of the Standard Industrial Classification The sample subdivided by industrial order and whether using or not using tests is given in Figure 11:1.

From this and other checks on representativeness detailed in the full report, the firms in the sample were deemed to be reasonably representative of British industry and commerce and the individuals adequately representative of the membership of the IPM. There is

Figure 11:1 The sample by category of industry and use or nonuse of tests

	Individuals		Firms	
	Test users	Test non-users	Test users	Test non-users
1 Food, drink & tobacco	41	42	27	33
2 Chemical & allied industries	48	41	38	38
3 Engineering & electrical goods	106	89	85	82
4 Metal manufacture, shipbuilding & marine engineering vehicles, metal goods	39	41	33	34
5 Textiles, clothing & footwear	29	24	27	22
6 Agriculture, forestry, fishery, mining & quarrying bricks, pottery, glass, cement, timber, furniture, paper, printing, publishing, other manufacturing industries	60	53	39	53
7 Construction, gas, electricity, water, transport & communication, distributive trade	59	49	34	47
8 Insurance, banking & finance, miscellaneous services, public administration & defence	28	43	25	43
9 Professional & scientific services	13	23	13	23
Total	423	405	321	375

no way of knowing whether the proportion of the sample using tests is representative of British industry.

However, the information derived from the survey about

the use of tests in 321 British companies is more comprehensive than any previously available. The information about the intentions of 375 companies of using or not using tests in the future is also seen as being of value to companies thinking about introducing tests into the work of a personnel department or of extending present use.

USE OF TESTS

The analysis of the information supplied by respondents was intended to answer the following questions concerning test use and policy:

1 What elements at present made up the selection process?
2 How long have companies been using tests?
3 For what purposes were tests most frequently used?
4 What types of tests were most frequently used?
5 How many tests were used on a single occasion?
6 For what type of staff were tests used?
7 What specific tests were used?
8 Did firms who used tests carry out validation exercises?
9 Were firms at present using tests likely to extend their use?
10 Were firms not at present using tests likely to introduce them or not, and were the reasons for not using tests at present known?

Procedures constituting the selection process
This information was available for both test-user and non-user sectors of the sample.

For the purpose of the survey, six procedures were listed: application form, interview, medical report, references, formal qualifications, psychological or aptitude tests. The information is summarized in Figure 11:2 where the frequency of each procedure for the six main types of staff is presented.

This information was collected in such a way that it was possible to ascertain how many procedures were used for each type of staff. The range, across staff types, was from one to six in the user group and one to five (by definition) in the non-user group.

For some types of staff in both groups the maximum number of procedures was involved, while for others only one was reported. (User firms did not use tests for all types of staff so there is no anomaly here.)

Figure 11.2 Selection procedures (as percentages)

	Managers/ supervisors		Professional technical		Clerical & sales		Technicians		Craftsmen		Operatives	
	Users	Non-users	Users	Non-users	Users	Non-users	Users	Non-users	Users	Non-users	Users	Non-users
Application form	89	81	91	82	91	85	83	75	80	65	79	65
Interview	94	88	95	88	94	91	85	79	84	74	86	77
Medical report	58	39	58	40	56	36	53	36	54	33	54	34
References taken up	72	71	73	71	67	66	54	52	42	35	39	32
Formal qualifications	51	49	81	75	22	16	51	47	32	27	5	5
Psychological tests	27	–	32	–	50	–	36	–	45	–	32	–

For summary purposes a comparison is made of firms using five or more procedures in each part of the sample. The information is summarized in Figure 11:3.

Figure 11:3 Frequency of use of number of selection procedures (as percentages)

Number of procedures	Managers/ supervisors		Professional/ technical		Clerical/ sales	
	Users	Non-users	Users	Non-users	Users	Non-users
1 or 2	5	10	5	4	8	18
3 or 4	46	63	35	57	52	70
5 or 6	49	27	60	39	40	12

Number of procedures	Technicians		Craftsmen		Operatives	
	Users	Non-users	Users	Non-users	Users	Non-users
1 or 2	5	14	8	29	17	40
3 or 4	48	61	51	56	63	55
5 or 6	47	25	41	15	20	5

The main conclusion to be drawn from Figures 11:2 and 11:3 is that firms which use tests as part of their selection procedure tend to be more thorough and comprehensive.

Length of time tests have been used
The use of tests ranged from a few months to 33 years, with just under 50 per cent of the use having begun in the previous 5 years. 33 per cent of the firms had been using tests between 5 and 15 years and the remainder for more than 16 years. The length of use within the different industrial categories was similar to the total group, except for chemical and allied industries and the professional category, with more of the former and fewer of the latter beginning use within the last 5 years. More firms employing between 100 and 999 employees have begun to use tests in the past 5 years. More than half the longest users are among the largest firms.

Purposes for which tests are used
As anticipated, tests were used mainly for initial

selection. Just under half the firms were using tests only for selection while only 11 firms (3 per cent) did not use tests at all for selection. The use of tests for selection, transfer and promotion was reported by 15 per cent. The food and agriculture subcategories make less use of tests for selection alone than does the total sample, while the construction and professional categories make more use of tests for this purpose. The full range of use is found in all industrial groups except insurance.

Types of test used
The questionnaire was limited to two sides of a single sheet and so less than complete information could be collected. The information about types of cognitive or reasoning test was classified into general ability or intelligence tests, mechanical ability, spatial ability, clerical, and manual dexterity. Measures of personal characteristics were grouped into personality and interest categories.

In the simplest case, a firm might use only one test for one category of staff. In other cases, up to seven major types of test could be used and, within each type, a different test could be used for one or more categories of staff. A first check was the number of different tests used within each of the main subcategories irrespective of type of staff.

General ability: intelligence tests 51 per cent of all test users (162 firms) employ a single general-ability test, another 11 per cent (34 firms) employ two tests, while only two firms report using as many as five different tests. Altogether, ability tests were used by 66 per cent of firms. Metal manufacture and agriculture are the subcategories with higher than average use of a single test, while construction and professional make less frequent use of a single ability test. The firms using two or more tests are found in all industrial groups.

Mechanical ability tests The situation is similar to that for general-ability tests, with the majority of firms using only one test. The total use of mechanical tests is less than that of general ability tests. 102 firms (32 per cent) report using one test and only three firms use two. No firm uses more than two.

Most use of mechanical tests is made in engineering and

electrical and metal manufacture. The apparently very low usage of mechanical tests in agriculture and textiles is somewhat surprising.

Spatial ability tests In all, 60 firms (19 per cent) make use of a spatial test, but only three use more than one such test. With the exception of food and drink and insurance, spatial tests are used by some firms within each industrial group. The frequency of use ranges from one firm in the professional and scientific services, to 22 firms in engineering and electrical.

Clerical tests Clerical tests are used about as often as are spatial tests: 58 firms (18 per cent) using one clerical test and seven firms (2 per cent) using two tests. When the use of clerical tests is considered in relation to the industrial categories wide variations are found, ranging from 11 per cent to 36 per cent. The maximum use is in the area where it might be expected - banking and insurance - but at the same time the occurrence might be seen as lower than would be anticipated in a basically clerical industry. The firms using two different clerical tests are to be found in all but two industrial groups.

Manual dexterity tests Just over 14 per cent (45) of all test users report using a single manual dexterity test, while a further 3.5 per cent (11) use two or more tests.
The users of manual dexterity tests are found in all industrial groups, other than professional and scientific services. The frequency of use ranges from one insurance firm, to 19 engineering and electrical firms.

Interest and personality measures As anticipated, assessment of personal characteristics was least often carried out. Only 23 firms (7 per cent) reported any use and only five (2 per cent) used more than one technique. With the exception of textiles and clothing, at least two firms in each category reported the use of interest/ personality measures. The highest frequency, of four firms, was in insurance and engineering.

Other tests
Altogether, there were 107 entries in the 'other' tests group which could not be classified into one of the main groups. The largest category was that of educational tests, which were used by 10 per cent. Educational tests are used in all industrial categories except professional

and scientific services.

24 firms indicated they used other tests, but the nature of the tests was not specified. Another nine firms reported using their own tests, but again did not indicate the nature of the tests.

The incidence of other classifiable tests was quite low, ranging from 4 to 11 firms (1 to 3.5 per cent). Fifteen firms were using tests for computer personnel and five were using tests for punch-card operators and, of these, only five firms indicated they were testing both categories of staff. Seven firms reported using either the National Institute of Industrial Psychology Engineering or Birkbeck batteries. These were spread over five industrial categories and used by all but the smallest size of firm.

Four firms reported using trade tests and 11 mentioned tests that could not be classified, because they either were incompletely named or, if named, have not been traced by the author.

Extent to which tests are used
An attempt was made to find out how many types of test were used by a firm, but about 10 per cent did not answer this question. From the replies received, 38 per cent used only one type of test, 27 per cent two types, 17 per cent three types, 12 per cent four types, 3 per cent five types, and only three firms used six or seven types.

Types of staff for which tests are used
Two main analyses were carried out. First, for each type of staff, the number of different types of tests used was summarized and, second, the number of different types of staff for whom tests are used was analysed.

Managers and supervisors Of the 88 firms using tests in the assessment of managers and supervisors, 60 use only one type of test, while two firms use six types. 26 firms use between two and five different types of tests. Firms using only one test type are found in all the industrial groups except professional. Although only three firms in this group use tests with managers and supervisors, none of these uses less than four types of tests.

Professional and technical staff The use of one type of test only is less frequent for this category of staff, 61 of the 103 firms reporting this way. In the textiles group only one firm reports using tests with this type of staff, and then only one type of test.

Clerical and sales staff More firms use tests for clerical staff than for any other type of staff. Over half of the total sample use tests. 98 firms (61 per cent) use only one type of test, a further 29 firms (25 per cent) use two tests, the remainder use between three and seven types of tests. The one firm reporting the use of seven different types was in engineering and electrical.

Technicians The pattern for the previous staff types changes with technicians, in that just 59 (50 per cent) of the 117 firms using tests for this purpose employ only one type. A further 26 firms (22 per cent) use two and another 20 (17 per cent) use three. The remainder use up to six different types.

Craftsmen The trend for using more than one type of test is continued with craftsmen. 42 per cent (61 firms) of the 144 firms selecting craftsmen employ a single test type. Two types are used by 41 firms (28 per cent), three by 26 (18 per cent). The remainder use between four and six types of test.

With the exception of the insurance and professional groups, at least five firms in each industrial group use tests to select craftsmen and some firms in each group use more than one type of test. The most extensive use of several types of tests is found in engineering, metal manufacture and construction which, because of their engineering aspects with long-term training periods, would be most likely to use comprehensive techniques.

Operatives The number of firms reporting the selection of operatives with the assistance of tests is lower than for the other 'practical' grades of staff, there being only 104. Moreover, the trend towards comprehensive use of tests is reversed and 59 per cent (61) use only one test type. Two tests are used by 31 firms (30 per cent), while the remaining 12 firms use either three or four types. Firms reporting the use of three or four types of tests are to be found in six of the nine industry categories.

Range of staff types for which companies use tests
If tests are used for all types of employees this would seem to be reasonably indicative of a firm seeing tests as an integral part of the selection process. On the other hand, if used with only one type of staff, tests

are presumably seen as contributing something special for that particular type.

The range is from one type of staff to all types: 77 firms (24 per cent) use tests for a single type of staff only, while 6 (2 per cent) use tests with all seven types of employees. The most frequently reported use is with two types, 86 firms (21 per cent). The frequency of usage decreases as the number of staff types increases: 60 use tests with three types, 31 with four, 26 with five and 12 with six. These figures are not unexpected, for the testing of managers and operatives is much less common than for other groups and that for professional and technical staff somewhat slower in developing.

The full range of staff types is only likely to be found in manufacturing and similar industries, and not in banking, insurance or professional services. The full range of testing is reported only in chemical and engineering and electrical, bricks and construction groups. Although the manufacturing industries do use tests with a wider range of staff, the distribution within these industrial groups is approximately the same as that for the total sample.

Specific tests used
The information on this point was the least complete. Respondents had been asked to name tests and to indicate numbers tested with each in the previous year. Assembling this information could well have posed problems for some companies. The most widely used ability tests were those distributed by NIIP, followed by Raven's Progressive Matrices, AH4, Differential Test Battery, AH5, Differential Aptitude Test, Otis, Primary Mental Abilities. In the mechanical test field, NIIP tests were again predominant, followed by Bennett Mechanical Comprehension, Differential Test Battery, ACER Mechanical Comprehension, ACER Mechanical Reasoning, Macquarrie, and Differential Aptitude Test.

Only three spatial tests were reported - NIIP, Revised Minnesota Paper Form Board and the Differential Test Battery Shapes Test. In the clerical field, the General Clerical Test was most often reported, with the ACER Speed and Accuracy and the Minnesota Checking Tests next. The NIIP Clerical Test is composed of a number of parts which were not clearly reported on. From NIIP staff it was ascertained that a sizeable number of each part is used.

On the personal characteristics side, the Cattell 16PF

was most often reported, with the Kuder and Rothwell vocational interest measures being mentioned equally often.

Over the whole field 63 different tests were mentioned by name, many by only one firm.

Evaluation of tests

All the information that could be mustered both in Britain and in the United States indicated that one of the last things to be done by users of tests for predictive purposes was to evaluate their effectiveness. It was therefore not surprising to find that only 61 firms (19 per cent) reported any form of evaluation. In some cases, this could mean a comprehensive, statistical assessment of several tests for different categories of employee. In other cases it could mean a semi-subjective report on one test for one category of worker. From the firms which reported evaluation having taken place, further information as sought by means of an additional letter containing specific questions. Less than half these firms returned the information and, of those who did, nearly all had conducted what must be termed an impressionistic study and not the conventional correlational or expectancy table analysis.

Reasons for not using tests

Six specific reasons which might, individually or in concert, be the basis for a firm not using tests were listed in the questionnaire, as well as an 'other' category. Of the six, 'managerial policy' is a blanket term, but in the course of discussion with IPM members on testing courses, it became clear that in some firms the staff did not know the basis of the nonuse, other than that it was 'policy'. This reason was the third most frequent, being given by 29 per cent (117) of the testnonuser group. Satisfaction with the present procedures and the lack of trained personnel to administer tests or, if trained, with time to do so, were given by 43 per cent of the group. Shortage of labour was noted by 26 per cent (107) as a reason. Whether other respondents were from areas where no labour shortages existed or whether they realized that, even with labour shortages, testing could effectively be used as part of the selection process will remain unknown.

INFORMATION ABOUT INDIVIDUAL MEMBERS OF THE IPM

While the information concerning firms was the most

pertinent, that concerning the individual members was also interesting. It could answer questions such as:

1 How many IPM members have been trained to use tests and have used them?
2 Do IPM members think tests are important or worthwhile?
3 What types of test would they wish to be trained to use?
4 Have IPM members been trained to interview?

The detailed analysis of these points is too lengthy for inclusion here but the conclusions are mentioned in the following summary.

SUMMARY AND IMPLICATIONS

Of the many findings in this study, those that seem of most general interest are:

1 The sample of 828 members (10.3 per cent of IPM UK membership in 1968) included 423 working in firms where tests were used.
2 The members were drawn from 696 firms, of which 321 report some use of psychological tests. To some readers, this will be the first unexpected result. As the beginning of the study, the modal number suggested was a 'handful' of firms. Those closer to test training expected more. It is not suggested, nor is there yet any watertight way of checking, that the proportion of 5:6 would hold throughout industry. However, it can be stated with confidence that the present ratio is closer to that in the sample than it is to the figure reported in the British Institute of Management survey of 1963.
3 If the trend of increasing use of tests as part of the selection process continues, some firms not at present using tests will find a nucleus of staff trained in the use of tests already in the post.
4 Training in test use has been of variable nature and quality. It clearly needs attention in some cases if the best use is to be made of tests. Some members had attended 3 or more courses but the majority had had only one course and often this was of an *ad hoc* nature. Appendix 1, which gives the guidelines drawn up by the British Psychological Society, indicates the basic requirements for adequate basic courses.
5 When asked about other training desired, the areas of personality and motivation assessment and the develop-

ment of criterion measure were most often mentioned.
6 Over three-quarters of test-user and non-user respondents favoured the use of tests with some categories of staff while 20 and 10 per cent respectively would favour the use of tests with all staff.
7 An unexpected result was the relatively high proportion of members who had had no training in interviewing: 21 per cent of those in test-user firms and 28 per cent of those in non-user firms.

POSTSCRIPT

The reader may well ask what changes have taken place since 1968. During that period, the Independent Assessment and Research Centre has been engaged on research, has undertaken assessment work which includes the use of tests, and has conducted an increasing number of courses on test use. It conducts these courses in its own right, jointly with the Institute of Personnel Management and within individual companies. In the six months before this book went to press, the Centre provided a speaker for meetings organized by the British Association for Commercial and Industrial Education, the British Institute of Management, the Industrial Society, an IPM Branch meeting and the Chartered Insurance Institute. All meetings were concerned with the contribution that psychological tests might make to personnel work.

From the Centre's own information, and from the increasing number of press references to the topic, it can be concluded that the area of personality testing is the one where most rapid increase in interest has taken place.

Increased use will not have matched increased interest, as the administration and interpretation of personality tests requires more stringent training than does the use of ability and aptitude tests. Nevertheless, one can report a growing use of personality tests and somewhat more rapid growth in the use of other tests.

With the increased use of tests one can appropriately conclude by reminding the interested reader that, while tests can make a useful contribution, the user must be adequately trained both to handle tests effectively and to keep the results in perspective with other available information.

REFERENCE

Miller, K.M. & Hydes, J. (1971), *The Use of Psychological Tests in Personnel Work* (London: Independent Assessment Research Centre)

Part Four

Appendices

APPENDIX 1

British Psychological Society: Criteria for evaluating short training courses on psychological tests

Those proposing the courses should furnish the following information to the Society whose agent in this matter is the Standing Committee on Test Standards.

1 Title of course
2 Name of organization offering course
3 Name of course director. The course director of member of staff responsible for day-to-day continuity should be a psychologist.
4 Aims - including designation of specific tests to be taught on the course. The class of course should be indicated in accordance with the British Psychological Society 1969 Document 'Classification of tests and test users' *Bulletin British Psychological Society*, vol 22, pp.109-11, 1969
5 Length of course
6 Type of student for whom course is intended, including prerequisite training, experience or qualifications.
7 Maximum number of students to be enrolled
8 Contents - syllabus - ethics of test use
9 Methods - lectures, tutorials, practical
10 Staff - names, qualifications, experience in testing, degree of participation in course.
   (a) It is particularly important that the degree of

    participation of each member of staff should
    be indicated.
  (b) Experience, both in test use and in training
    others to use tests, is essential for tutors.
  (c) Lectures on psychological topics should normally
    be provided by psychologists, i.e. persons eligible for graduate membership of the British
    Psychological Society. In all other cases qualification for giving lectures must be made clear.
11 Accommodation and facilities available
12 Assessment - theoretical, practical
13 Follow-up of students

The full statement and related documents may be obtained from The Secretary, British Psychological Society, 18-19 Albemarle Street, London W1.

APPENDIX 2

Tests referred to in Part Two

Some tests are referred to by more than one author: in order to avoid repetition and so that the reader may have an overview of the section, most of the tests referred to in Part 2 are described briefly below.

The psychological profession restricts the term 'test' to describe instruments which have objectively correct answers, e.g. ability and aptitude tests. Devices which assess interests, motivation and personality are referred to by other terms such as questionnaires, blanks or scales. In this book, 'test' has been used more broadly to cover all fields.

Every test is accompanied by a manual giving data relating to reliability, validity and norms, i.e. the performances which are expected, based on the performances of a standard sample. These manuals must be carefully studied.

ACER Mechanical Reasoning Test
In this test mechanical reasoning is evaluated by means of mechanical problems shown in diagrams. The correct answer to the problems must be chosen from a number of alternatives.

ACER Speed and Accuracy Test
A test of perceptual-motor speed which requires the

testee to check pairs of numbers and names for similarity or differences. The function measured by the test is related to clerical, administrative, sales work and some manual tasks.

AH4, AH5, AH6
These are intelligence tests devised by Alice Heim at Cambridge. AH4 is suitable for groups, which may be of unselected adults or children over 10, and also for selected groups of somewhat below average intelligence.

AH5 and AH6 are suitable for groups of people who are likely to show above average intelligence, such as students, research workers, and potential entrants to universities, polytechnics or professions. AH6 is described specifically as designed for selection of candidates for admission to such institutions, including training colleges.

Allport-Vernon-Lindzey Study of Values
This is designed to show the relative importance in personality organization of six interests or motives: the theoretical, economic, aesthetic, social, political and religious. A British revision is available.

Contact Personality Factor
An introversion-extraversion questionnaire.

EITS Clerical Test 1
A number and name checking test.

EPI Eysenck Personnel Inventory
Prepared by Professor H.J. Eysenck and based originally, but not entirely, on long experience with the Maudsley Personality Inventory. Gives a measure of extraversion (sociability, impulsiveness, preoccupation with externals), introversion (thoughtfulness, preoccupation with own ideas) and neuroticism (instability). All descriptions of factors can only be approximate. This test includes a measure designed to show how far a candidate is distorting his answers in his own favour.

Flanagan Industrial Tests (FIT)
A battery of 18 short tests: arithmetic, assembly, components, coordination, electronics, expression, ingenuity, inspection, judgment and comprehension, mathematics and reasoning, mechanics, memory, patterns, planning, precision, scales, tables and vocabulary.

A tester is unlikely to select more than three or four tests for any one position.

Gordon Surveys of Values
Each survey is designed to assess the importance of certain motivating factors. The interpersonal survey concerns six areas likely to be important in interacting with other people: support, conformity, recognition, independence, benevolence, leadership. The survey of personal values concerns areas likely to be seen as important for

an individual managing his own life.

Index Filing Test (prepared by IACC)
A short test of knowledge of the alphabet.

Maudsley Personality Inventory
See Eysenck Personality Inventory. The MPI is similar, but does not include a measure of distortion.

Moray House Adult Intelligence Test 1
This is a carefully researched test of adult intelligence, balanced in its emphasis on different aspects of intelligence, with high reliability and demonstrated validity.

NIIP Tests
These are confined to those authorized by the NIIP to use them. The National Foundation for Educational Research, Windsor, now deals with qualifications of testers. The tests referred to in this book are tests of verbal and general intelligence of high reliability and demonstrated validity.

PTI Verbal Test
One of the Personnel Tests for Industry produced by the Psychological Corporation Staff who state it yields a reliable measure of general mental ability in a short time.

Revised Minnesota Paper Form Board Test (RMPFB)
This is a paper-and-pencil test of the special ability known as 'spatial perception'. The candidate is required to show how two-dimensional shapes can be assembled into a complete design. This ability is related to engineering and artistic design and other areas where the mental manipulation of shapes and form is required.

Rothwell-Miller Interest Blank
A vocational interest measure which establishes an order of preference for 12 fields of work.

Self-analysis Questionnaire
A short questionnaire to assess anxiety.

16PF Sixteen Personality Factor Questionnaire
A widely used personality test produced by the Institute for Personality and Ability Testing under the direction of Professor R.B.Cattell. It yields measures on 16 primary personality factors which are designated by letters. A low measure on each factor has approximately the meaning indicated below on the left, while a high measure has approximately the meaning indicated below on the right. A 10-point scale is used.

Factor	Meaning of Low Score (1)	Meaning of High Score (10)
A	Cool, aloof	Warm, helpful
B	Concrete-thinking	Abstract-thinking
C	Emotional	Realistic, controlled
E	Submissive	Dominant, assertive

Factor	Meaning of Low Score (1)	Meaning of High Score (10)
F	Quiet	Effervescent, talkative
G	Expedient	Conscientious, persevering
H	Shy, retiring	Bold, venturesome
I	Down-to-earth	Sensitive, demanding
L	Trusting	Suspicious
M	Practical	Imaginative, inventive
N	Natural, naive	Sophisticated, calculating
O	Placid, calm	Anxious
Q1	Conservative	Radical
Q2	Group-dependent	Independent of others
Q3	Weak, vacillating	Purposeful
Q4	Relaxed	Tense

By combining the primary factors, variously weighted, second-order and criterion dimensions have been found including: general anxiety, exvia (similar to extraversion), tough poise, independence, leadership, creativity and potential as a researcher. In each case the approximate meaning of the high score is mentioned here, so that the low score means the opposite, e.g. the low score on the exvia scale means invia (similar to introversion).

In the 16PF, as with all such questionnaires, the author has provided a comprehensive, specific definition of each scale. *The key words here are only partial definitions.* Reference to the test handbook is *essential* to gain a full understanding of the nature of the dimensions.

Thurstone Interest Schedule
This compares the strengths of interests in the following fields: physical science, biological science, computational work, business, executive, persuasive, linguistic, humanitarian, artistic and musical work.

Thurstone Test of Mental Alertness
A test of verbal and quantitative ability in which the alternation of different types of item is planned to test the capacity of the individual to switch set and is an important factor in gaining a high score.

Short Tests of Clerical Ability (STCA)
These are single-sheet tests covering seven aspects of clerical ability: business vocabulary, coding, checking, filing, language, arithmetic, directions.
The tester can choose the combination most relevant for his purposes.

Other tests used are adequately described in the text in which their use is discussed.
Where questionnaires or attitude tests not included in the above descriptions are referred to in the text,

specially constructed questionnaires or attitude tests were used, unless otherwise indicated.

Index

Ability and aptitude tests 112-13
   see also under Clerical
Ability Block (Morrisby DTB) 97-6
Acceptance of, or declining, a job
   offer, tests for determining pro-
   bability of 72-4
ACER Mechanical Comprehension Test 161
ACER Mechanical Reasoning Test
   NRC 139, 141-3
   BIC 161, 171
ACER Speed and Accuracy Test 62, 80
   111, 161, 171
Administrators of tests, training of
   Post Office 41-2
   courses in test taking ability 12-13
AH4 Test (Alice Heim's) 53-4, 58, 59,
   92, 139-41, 161, 172
AH5 Test (Alice Heim's) 161, 172
AH6 Test (Alice Heim's) United
   Biscuits 48, 59, 64, 172
Allport-Vernon-Lindzey, Study of
   Values, Test 79, 81, 172
Alphabet, knowledge of, test for,

Clerical posts 111
Anastasi (1968) 8
Anxiety, tests throwing up 111
APEX (trade union) 19
Aptitudes, tests revealing special 31
Arithmetic Tests 111, 116-20
  see also under Numerical
Assessment Centres 49-50
Assessors of tests, training of
    41-2

Beaton, R. 137-48
Bennett Mechanical Comprehension Test
    161
BEST Test (Basic Employee Selection
    Test) 5
Biographical data on salesmen 79
Biological scientists, GAT profile
    combinations of 96
Birkbeck batteries 159
Bray, Dr Douglas 35
Bray and Moses (1972) 71
British Association for Commercial
    and Industrial Education 164
British Industry and Commerce, tests
    used in 151-64
  description of sample 152-4
  use of tests, 154-62
    procedures in selection process
      154-6
    length of time tests have been used
      156
    purposes for which tests used
      156-7
    types of test used 157
    general ability and intelligence
      tests 157
    mechanical ability tests 157-58
    spatial ability test 158
    clerical tests 158
    manual dexterity tests 158
    interest and personality measures 158
    other tests 158-60
    extent tests are used 159
    types of staff for which tests
      used 159

   managers and supervisors 159
   professional and technical staff
     159-60
   clerical and sales staff 160
   technicians 160
   craftsmen 160
   operatives 160
   range of staff involved 160-1
   specific tests used 161-2
   evaluation of tests 162
   reasons for not using tests 162
  information about individual members
    of IPM 162-3
  summary and implications 163-4
  postcript 164
British Institute of Management 152
British Psychological Society 163, 169-70
Burt, Sir Cyril 20
Byham and Spitzer (1971) 14

Campbell and Campbell (1970) 77
Campbell *et al.* (1970) 71, 131
Career Interest Test (Morrisby's) 99
Cattell, James McKeen 151
Cattell 16 Personality Factor (PF)
  Questionnaire 6, 62, 65, 79-80, 127,
    128-30, 173
Cattell 16 Personality Factor (PF)
   Test 7, 48, 53-4, 56, 58, 63-4
   72-3, 81, 146, 161-2
  see also Forms A-D, 16 PF Tests
Cattell *et al.* (1970) 69-70
Central Training Council 152
Chi-square 139, 145
City and Guild Qualifications 39
Civil Rights Act (USA-1964) 13-14
Civil Service Selection Board (CISB) 35
Clerical accuracy test 111
Clerical skills, test for 31, 56, 158
Clerical post selections, choosing tests
   for 109-21
  purposes of the study 109-11
  samples 110-12
  criterion measures 112
  contribution of each individual
    test 112-16
    ability and aptitude tests 112-13

measures of personal value 114-16
most suitable combination of tests
     116-19
        in insurance work 116-18
        in mail order work 118-19
    effectiveness 119-21
    conclusion 121
    for British Industry and Commerce 160
Coding test, STCA 111, 116, 118
Commerce (British), tests used in,
    see British Industry and Commerce
Complaints in telephone service, validation
    of tests used to select people to deal
    with 36
Compound Series Test (CST) 94, 96
Comptometer operators 23
Computerisation of test results 143
Computing equipment and staff 39-40
    56, 58, 59, 96, 159
    see also Programming jobs
Concept speed test 96
Copeland, J. 91-107
Counselling situations 99, 103
Courses in test-invigilating ability
    12-13
Craftsmen, tests for 160
Criterion
    need to establish a 25-7, 112
    for a national retail company 139-47
Criteria, measurement of
    salesmen 79
    for evaluation of short training
        courses on psychological tests
        (British Psychological Society)
        169-70
Cronback (1973) 65
CST, see Compound Series Test

Decisions, making, using tests for
    10-11
*Declining, or acceptance of, a job offer,
    tests to determine probability of
    72-4
Dexterity measurement (Morrisby DTB)
    94, 97
    see also Manual dexterity tests

180

Differential Aptitude Test 161
Differential Test Battery 5, 97-99
    103-7, 161
Differential Test Battery Shapes Test
    161
Directors, taking tests by, encouraged
    United Biscuits 58
Distortion, tests to uncover 7-8
Dixon (1971) 73
Drenth (1971) 71
DTB, see Differential Test Battery

EITS Clerical 1 Test 111, 172
Electronic firms, selection for engineers
    for, see Engineers, selection of, for
    electronic firms
Eleven-plus selection 21
Engineering Trade Test 139
Engineers, selection of, for electronic
    firms 91-107
  Morrisby Differential Test Battery
  93-99
    ability block 95-6
    modal profile 96-7
    dexterity 97
    whole profile 97-99
    summary 99
  other tests 99-100
  using the tests 100-3
    training 101-3
    supervision 103
    counselling 103
  contribution from DTB 105-6
    recruitment and selection 104-5
    interviewing technique 105-6
    training methods 106
  future plans 106
  conclusion 106-7
English language usage test 111
  see also Language; Word Fluency test
Ethics and other professional considerations
    12-15
Evaluation tests 70-5
Expectancy charts 139-40
Eysenck Personality Inventory Test
    6, 7, 80, 127, 128, 130-1 172

Faking personality tests 65
Filing tests, *see* Index filing tests
Fisher Exact Probability Test 73
FIT Arithmetic Test 111, 172
Flanagan Industrial Tests (FIT) 111, 172
Forcible choice questions 65
Forms A-D, 16PF Tests 59, 127, 128, 130
  see also Cattell 16PF Questionnaire;
    Cattell 16PF Test
Furness, W.A. 29-45

Galton, Sir Francis 151
Gas salesmen 81-6
GAT profile combinations 94, 96
General Ability Tests
  BIC 157
  GAT-P 94
  verbal 5
  see also Verbal ability, tests for;
    Verbal tests
General Clerical Test 161
Geographical factors affecting
    selection decisions 138
Ghiselli (1966) 9
Gibson, J. 122-35
Goode (1969) 99
Goodness of Fit Index (Cattell's)
    69
Gordon's Personal Profile Test 6
Graduate selection 61-75
  selection provedure 63
  current testing procedure 63-4
  problems encountered 64-6
  line managers' reactions to tests 66
  graduates' reaction 66-69
  motivational distortion 69-70
  evaluation of tests 70-5
  summary 75
Graduates
  attitude of, to tests 22, 25
  recruitment from Post Office 30, 33
  United Biscuits 48-9, 56, 59
Guildford-Zimmerman Temperament
    Survey 6
Guion (1963) 78, (1965) 5, 63, 70

Harcourt Brace Jovanovich (a USA
    distribution company) 151- 2
Heim, Alice, *et al.* (1970) 64
  see also AH4, AH5, and AH6 tests
Higham, T.M. 19-28
Hobbies, importance of, when
    selecting salesmen 81

Idea-tional Fluency Test 96
Independent Assessment and Research
    Centre 164
Index filing test 111, 116-18, 173
Industry (British)
  table of users and non-users of
    tests by categories 153
  see also British Industry and
  Commerce, tests used in
Ingleton, C.C.P. 61-75
Institute of Personnel Management
    152, 162-3, 164
Insurance work, tests for 110-19
    116-18
Intellectual skills 38-9
Intelligence/Mental Alertness Test
    111
Intelligence, test for 4-5, 31
  for British industry and
    commerce 157
Interests
  extent of personal, importance of,
    81
  tests for British industry 158
  to establish personal 5-6
Interpersonal Values Survey Test
    111
Interview panels, composition of 64
Interviews
  by two-man teams 32-3
  disadvantages of 3-4
  need for, as well as tests 28
  time allotted for 48
  for electronic engineers 105-6
Introduction of tests
  four important steps for the 20
  experiences of United Biscuits 57-59

IPM *see* Institute of Personnel
    Management

Job-relatedness (of tests) 11
King Alfred, HMS intelligence tests
    at 24
Kuder and Rothwell Vocational
    Interest Measures 162

Language tests, STCA 111
  see also Word Fluency Tests
Lawshe and Balma (1966) 5, 139
Line managers encouraged to understand
    nature of tests 47
Local authority staff, use of tests
    for 122-35
  inherrent difficulties 122-3
  decision to use tests 123-4
  purposes for which tests used 125
  staff assessed 125-6
  tests and their contribution 127-32
    tests used 127
    evaluation of test contribution 127-28
    16PF Questionnaire 128-30
    Eysenck Personality Inventory 130-1
    NIIP tests 131-2
    Moray House Adult Intelligence
      test No.1 132
    summary 132
    future developments 133-5

Macquarrie Test 161
McReynolds (1971) 71
Mail order work, tests for 110, 118-19
Management development, tests for 49-51
Management potential, early identification of 33-4
Manager, typical example of a report
    on 51-2
Manual dexterity
  tests in general 5
  for British industry and commerce 158
  for electronic engineers 94, 97
Married women 109
Maudsley Personality Inventory 80, 173

Mechanical Ability Tests 157-58
MECHanical Tests 94, 96
Medical Research Council's Unit of
   Social and Applied Psychology 59
Memory, tests for 5
Mental alertness verbal tests 111
Mental Behaviour Test (modal profile) 94
Miller, K.M. 3-14, 109-21, 151-65
Minnesota Checking Tests 161
Minnesota Paper Form Board Tests (revised)
   (RMPFB)
  national retail companies 139, 143, 173
  British industry and commerce 161.
Modal profile (Morrisby DTB) 94, 96-98
Moore (1969) 92
Moore and Hartman (1931) 77
Moray House Adult Intelligence Test
   No.1, (LA) 132, 173
Morrisby (1955) 92
Morrisby Career Interest Test 99
Morrisby Differential Test Battery
   93-99
  see also Differential Test Battery
Morrisby Personal Questionnaire 99
Motivation, tests to establish 5-6
Motor dexterity tests 5

National Foundation for Educational
   Research (NFER) 92, 131, 151
National Instutute of Industrial
   Psychology, see NIIP
National Retail Companies, see
   Telefusion, Limited
NIIP, organization of, and tests
   supplied by 59, 127, 131-2, 151,
   159, 161, 173
Numerical and Perceptual Test
   (GAT-N) 94
Numerical Ability Test 111
Numerical skills, tests for 31-2
  see also Arithmetic Test

Objectivity of tests 8
Oil, salesmen for 87-88
Oil, company, tests for, see Graduate
selection

Omnibus tests 4-5
ONC courses 107
Operatives, tests for 160
Opposition to tests, overcoming 20-2, 57-8
Optimum Performance Tests 65-6, 75
Organizational factors of salesmen 79
Otis Test 5, 80, 161

Paper and pencil tests 21, 62
Paterson 20
Pear, Professor Tom 20
Perceptual Tests (GAT-N) 5, 94
Perfectionists 101-2
Persistence in salesmen 85
Personality, tests to assess 6-7
  for oil company 65
  for British industry and commerce 158
Personality Factor, see Cattell Personality Factor 16 Questionnaire-Cattell Personality Factor 16 Tests
Personal value, measures of 114-16
Personnel Officer's method of conducting tests 45-6
Phi coefficients 112, 118, 119, 139
Post Office Appointments Centre 30
Post Office Corporation, use of tests in 29-45
  tests for postmen 29-30
  reasons for using 30-1
  below-management levels tests 31-2
  management levels, tests for 32-4
  tests for promotion 34, 35
  Assessment Centre, concept of 30, 34-5
  current uses of tests 34-6
  validation 36-40
    at management level 37-9
    below management level 39-41
  tests in use 41-5
    training 41-2
    security arrangements 42-3
    is one version enough 43
    standards of scoring 43
    achieving acceptability 43-4

presentation of validation
  studies 44-5
Preservation test 96
Primary Mental Abilities Test 161
Problems involving psychological
  tests in oil company 64-6
Procedures adopted when testing
  salesmen 79
Product knowledge in salesmen 85
Professional qualification holders
  22, 25
 see also under Graduates
Professioal staff, tests for
  British inuustry and commerce
  159-61
Profile interpretation 93-4
Programming jobs 23, 96
 see also Computing equipment and staff
Promotion, tests for Post Office, 34, 35
Psychologically qualified, an
 essential when giving successful
   tests 27-8
Psychological testing, methods, and
   evaluation of 1-15
 for general ability or intelligence 4-5
 for special abilities 5
 for specific interests and motivation
   5-6
 for assessment of personality 6-7
 for distortion 7-8
 characteristics of 8-9
   objectivity 8
   reliability 8
   validity 8-9
 using results 9-10
 making decisions 10-11
 how to introduce 11-12
 professional and ethical considerations
   12-15
Psychological tests, case studies in
   use of 19-28
 overcoming initial opposition 20-2
 acceptability 22
 technical soundness 22-4
 validation must be repeated 24-5
 establishing a criterion 25-6

the classic approach 27
hints on using tests 27-8
Psychometric data on salesmen 78-9
PTI Verbal Test 111, 116-18
    120, 146, 173
Punch operators 23, 32, 39, 159

Qualifications to conduct tests 12
Questionnaires
  for selecting salesmen, *see* Salesmen
    selection
  self-report type 6, 111, 173
  vocational interest 5

Randell, G.A. 77-90
Raven's Progressive Matrices 5, 62
    64, 80, 161
Reasoning tests 38-9
Recruitment
  Post Office 29-30
  electronic engineers 104-5
Reliability of tests 8
Research project into selection of
    graduates, *see* Graduate Selection
Residential staff 125
Results of tests, how to use 9-10
  professional and ethical matters
    and 12-15
Retail companies, *see* Telefusion
    Limited
RMPFB, *see* Minnesota Paper Form
    Board (revised)
Rodger, Professor Alec. 21
Rorschach Ink Blot Test 6
Rosenzveig Picture-Frustration
    Study 80
Rothwell-Miller Interest Blank
  electronic engineers 99, 173
  clerical posts 111
Rowntree, Seebolm 19-20
Rowntree, Limited 19-28 *passim*
Salesmen
  are they born or trained? 77-79
  selection of, use of tests and
    scored questionnaires for 77-90
      collecting the data 78-9

    tests and questionnaires used
      79-80
    analysing the data 80
    findings and outcomes 80-88
    for gas 81-6
    as tyremen 86-7
    as oilmen 87
  general conclusions 88-90
  suitable tests for 24-5, 56
  see also Sales staff *below*
Sales staff, tests for British
    industry and commerce 160
  see also Salesmen *above*
Scatterbrains 101
Scattergrams 139
Schein (1970) 70
Schmidt and Kaplan (1974) 71
Science Research Associates (USA)
    151
Scoring, standards of 43
Screening techniques
  tests used to reduce number of
    interviewees 30, 56
  to select managers 33
Security arrangements (of test doc-
    uments)
  Post office 42-3
  United Biscuits 58
Selection prodedure
  British industry and commerce
    154-6
  electronic engineers 99-100
  oil 63
  Local authorities 122-35
  national retail companies 137-48 *passim*
Self-analysis Form 111, 173
SHAPES test for electronic
    engineers 94-6
  for British industry and
    commerce 161
Siegel (1956) 73
Sixteen PF Tests, *see under* Cattell
Social case workers 125
Solitary workers 101
Spatial ability test 158, 161
Special abilities, tests for 6

Speed
  tests to ascertain 5
  and accuracy tests 31-2
  see also ACER Speed and Accuracy
    Tests
Spelling, DTB tests throw up man poor
    at 102-3
Status-conscious persons 101
STCA Arithmetic Test 111, 116
STCA Coding Test 111, 116, 118
STCA Language Test 111
Sten scores, supervisors 53-4
Strong Vocational Interest Block 80
Study of Values (Allport-Vernon-
    Lindzey's) 79, 81, 172
success-conscious persons 101
Supervisors
  importance of, to understand
    subordinates 103
  selection of 52-6
  tests for 159
  for Local authorities 125
Survey of Personal Values Tests
    111, 114-16

Technical staff, tests for 159-60
Technicians, tests for 160
Telefusion, Limited, use of tests
    at 137-48
  factors influencing introduction
    137-38
  objectives 138-9
  criterion 139-47
    where one only suitable 139-42
    when not categorical but con-
    tinuous 142-3
    where more than one 143-5
    where personality 'suited' to
      a job 145-7
contribution made by tests to sel-
    ection prodedure 147-8
Telephonists, special aptitudes for
Tests and questionnaires for sales-
    men selection 79-80
Tests

by groups, used for clerical posts 111
  characteristics of 8-9
  current use of 35-6
  early types of, in use at
     Rowntrees, Limited 21
  five categories of in use 31
  procedures 45-6
     see also Selection procedure
  for clerical selection, *see* Clerical post selections
  for Local authorities, *see* Local authority staff, use of tests for
  hints on using 27-8
  how to introduce 11-12, 20, 57-9
  in British Industry and Commerce
  see British Industry and Commerce, tests used in
  three or more variations of, to ensure fairness 43
  types of, available 6-8, 172-4
  used by Local authorities, tabled by staff categories 129
  use of by British industry and commerce 154
  table of 153, 154
Thurstone Interest Inventory 62, 79 81
Timetable
  for interviews 64
  for a selection programme, example of 48
Training
  for ability to supervise tests 12-13 41-2
  for Local authority staff 125
  in NRC, cost of 139
  supervisors of tests 41-2
  systematic, must be followed by systematic selection 28
Typing 23
  see also under Clerical
Tyre salesmen 86-7

Ungerson (1975) 8

United Biscuits, use of tests
   at 45-60
  procedure for testing during
    selection 45-6
  general approach by company to
    testing 46-7
  company policy 47-8
  graduate recruitment 48-9
  management development 49-52
    specimen report on manager 51-2
  supervisors, selection of 52-6
  other uses of tests 56-7
  introduction of tests 57-9
  conclusions 59-61

Validating tests 24-5, 26
Validity of tests
  in general 8-9
  for the Post Office 36-40, 42-3
Verbal tests
  in general 5, 31, 111
  GAT-V 94
Vocational Interest Tests 111
Vocation Interest Questionnaires 5

War Office Selection Boards
   (WOSBs) 35
Watson Glaser Critical Thinking
   Appraisal 59
Whole profile (Morrisby DTB) 97-99
Wilson, D. 45-60
Word Fluency Test 96
Written appraisal, importance of 35